D0453011

Victor W. Watton

Religion
and Society
Revision Guide
THIRD EDITION

HODDER
EDUCATION
AN HACHETTE UK COMPANY

Every effort has been made to trace all copyright holders, but if any have been inadvertently overlooked the Publishers will be pleased to make the necessary arrangements at the first opportunity.

Although every effort has been made to ensure that website addresses are correct at time of going to press, Hodder Education cannot be held responsible for the content of any website mentioned in this book. It is sometimes possible to find a relocated web page by typing in the address of the home page for a website in the URL window of your browser.

Hachette UK's policy is to use papers that are natural, renewable and recyclable products and made from wood grown in sustainable forests. The logging and manufacturing processes are expected to conform to the environmental regulations of the country of origin.

Orders: please contact Bookpoint Ltd, 130 Milton Park, Abingdon, Oxon OX14 4SB. Telephone: (44) 01235 827720. Fax: (44) 01235 400454. Lines are open 9.00–5.00, Monday to Saturday, with a 24-hour message answering service. Visit our website at www.hoddereducation.co.uk

© Victor W. Watton 2003
First published in 2003 by
Hodder Education,
An Hachette UK Company
338 Euston Road
London NW1 3BH

Second Edition published in 2007.
This Third Edition published in 2010.

Impression number	7
Year	2014

All rights reserved. Apart from any use permitted under UK copyright law, no part of this publication may be reproduced or transmitted in any form or by any means, electronic or mechanical, including photocopying and recording, or held within any information storage and retrieval system, without permission in writing from the publisher or under licence from the Copyright Licensing Agency Limited. Further details of such licences (for reprographic reproduction) may be obtained from the Copyright Licensing Agency Limited, Saffron House, 6–10 Kirby Street, London EC1N 8TS.

Cover photos l–r: © Mark Edwards/Still Pictures; © kipa/Corbis; © Neil Higginson/Rex Features.
Typeset in 12/14pt Electra LH Regular by Gray Publishing, Tunbridge Wells.
Printed in India

A catalogue record for this title is available from the British Library.

ISBN: 978 0340 975 657

Contents

Introduction

This book is designed to support your revision of the Edexcel GCSE Religious Studies Specification: Unit 8 Religion and Society based on the study of Christianity and one other religion.

Each section of the book covers one of the four sections of the GCSE specification. Each section begins with a list of the key words you need to learn. Then each sub-topic within the specification for that section is covered as a separate topic. Each topic:

- has a summary of the key points
- outlines the main points needed to answer the explain questions (question c)
- gives arguments for and against the issues raised by the topic to make it easier to answer the response questions (question b) and the evaluation questions (question d).

Each section finishes with guidance on how to answer exam questions and an end of section test.

The book also contains an appendix to give you guidance on self-marking the end of section tests and how to improve your performance on the section tests.

How to use the book

You should revise all the topics in Section 1. In Sections 2, 3 and 4, for the topics which are about the attitudes of another religion other than Christianity, you should only revise *one religion* from Islam, Judaism, Hinduism or Sikhism.

1 Learn a section at a time.
2 Learn the key words of a section.
3 Work through each topic in a section in this way:
    - learn the key points
    - learn the main points
    - learn the advice on how to answer evaluation questions.
4 When you have learned all eleven topics, do the end of section test.
5 Use the mark scheme from the Appendix to mark your test, and go through the guidance on how to improve your performance. If you find it difficult to self-mark the test, visit www.hoddereducation.co.uk/religionandsociety where there is a more specific mark scheme for each test.
6 Make sure you know everything about how to deal with the exam paper (see page 3 opposite) before you take the examination.

How to deal with the exam paper

1. When you go into the exam hall and find your desk, your exam paper should be face up on the desk. Before you are allowed to open the paper, you can complete the front cover by:
   - writing your surname in the first top box
   - writing your first names in the adjoining box (if there is not enough room, write initials for those that will not fit)
   - writing your centre number (this will be on display in the hall) in the first box below
   - writing your personal exam number (you will receive this from your school before the exam) in the adjoining box.

   It is important that you get all of these completely correct, otherwise someone else may get your mark and grade!

2. When you are told to start, make a note of the time. You have 22 minutes per question (you could work on – part a) 2 minutes, part b) 4 minutes, part c) 10 minutes, part d) 6 minutes). You should try not to go beyond this as you will lose marks on Section 4 if you run out of time.

3. Start on Section 1 by choosing one of the questions, *either the whole of* question 1 (parts a, b, c, d) or *the whole of* question 2 (parts a, b, c, d). You should decide on which question to choose by whether you can do parts c) and d) as these are worth 14 marks of the 20 available.

4. Make sure you read the question carefully before you answer it and highlight key words such as *why, how, some, others, choose one religion other than Christianity.*

5. Make sure you put a line through the box beside the question you have chosen at the top of the first answer page. Your answers will be scanned and put onto a website, and the examiner will only be marking specific questions. If you do not indicate which question you have answered, your answer may not be marked.

6. If you run out of space, ask for a supplementary sheet of paper. The scanner does not pick up any writing outside the margins!

7. If you have any time left:
   - check that you have answered every part of each question
   - go through each answer to part c) checking the spelling and grammar and trying to add some extra specialist vocabulary, e.g. could you use any of the key words?
   - go through each part d) answer checking that you have three reasons for each point of view and adding reasons where necessary.

Section 1 Rights and responsibilities

KEY WORDS FOR SECTION 1	
Bible	the holy book of Christians
Church	the community of Christians (with a small c it means a Christian place of worship)
Conscience	an inner feeling of the rightness or wrongness of an action
The Decalogue	the Ten Commandments
Democratic processes	the ways in which all citizens can take part in government (usually through elections)
Electoral processes	the ways in which voting is organised
The Golden Rule	the teaching of Jesus that you should treat others as you would like them to treat you
Human rights	the rights and freedoms to which everyone is entitled
Political party	a group which tries to be elected into power on the basis of its policies (e.g. Labour, Conservative)
Pressure group	a group formed to influence government policy on a particular issue
Situation Ethics	the idea that Christians should base moral decisions on what is the most loving thing to do
Social change	the way in which society has changed and is changing (and also the possibilities for future change)

Topic 1.1 The Bible as a basis for making moral decisions

Main points

Moral decisions are when you have to decide what is the right or wrong thing to do. A simple moral decision would be whether to give 50p to save a child from polio, or spend it on sweets. Most people need help in making such decisions.

Why many Christians use only the Bible when making a moral decision

- They believe that the **Bible** is the word of God and so is God's guidance to humans about how to make decisions.
- The Bible contains God's teachings on how Christians should behave. **The Decalogue**, for example, gives very clear guidance on such things as: the treatment of parents, stealing, murder, adultery, lying, etc.
- The Bible contains the teachings of Jesus on how to live. As Christians believe Jesus is the Son of God, they should follow his teachings about moral decision-making.
- The Bible contains letters from the leading disciples of Jesus about how Christians should behave. Christians believe that the writers of the letters knew Jesus and were guided by the Holy Spirit so their guidance must be important for Christians today.

Why some Christians do not think the Bible is the most important guide for making moral decisions

- Some Christians believe that the Bible was written by humans inspired by God, so many of its attitudes need to be changed for the modern world (for example, St Paul's attitude to women and slaves).
- Some Christians believe they need the **Church** to tell them what the Bible means for today.
- Other Christians would use their own **conscience** or reason to decide whether to follow the Bible today.

Key points

Some Christians would use only the Bible when making moral decisions because they believe that God speaks through the Bible. The Bible records God's teaching on how to behave and what Jesus taught about morality.

Evaluation questions

You may be required to argue for and against the Bible being the most important guide for making moral decisions.

1. To argue for, you should use the reasons above left on why many Christians use only the Bible when making moral decisions.

2. To argue against, you could use the reasons on the left on why some Christians do not think the Bible is the most important guide for making moral decisions.

Topic 1.2 The authority of the Church as a basis for making moral decisions

Key points

The Church has authority because Church leaders are in the best position to say what the Bible means for today, and they always give guidance on moral issues. The Church is the final authority for Catholic Christians because the Pope and the bishops are believed to have special powers in interpreting the Bible.

Main points

Although the Bible is the basic guide for Christian decision-making, most Christians believe that the Bible needs explaining to be used for life today. Many Christians believe that only the Church can do this because:

- They believe the Church is the Body of Christ – Jesus working in today's world – so it must have the same authority as Christ.
- Most Christians believe that God speaks to the world today through the Church.
- The Church is guided by God in making decisions on today's moral issues.
- Following the guidance of the Church stops Christians from being confused about what to do, and means Christians can be sure they are doing the right thing.
- Catholic Christians believe that the Magisterium (the Pope and the bishops interpreting the Bible and tradition for Catholics today) gives perfect guidance on moral behaviour.

Evaluation questions

You may be required to argue for and against following the teaching of the Church being the best basis for making moral decisions.

1. To argue for, you should use the reasons above.

2. To argue against, you could use the reasons for the Bible being more important (Topic 1.1, page 5), or conscience (Topic 1.3, page 7) or Situation Ethics (Topic 1.4, page 8).

Topic 1.3 The role of conscience as a guide in making moral decisions

Main points

All humans have a conscience which makes them feel guilty if they do things which they think are wrong. Some Christians believe they should follow the guidance of the Bible and the Church, but if their conscience tells them not to, they should follow their conscience.

Why some Christians believe they should follow their conscience

- They believe that the voice of conscience seems to be the same as the voice of God, therefore Christians should follow it.
- The Church says that Christians should follow their conscience as if it were the voice of God.
- St Paul and St Thomas Aquinas taught that Christians should use their conscience as the final part of moral decision-making, so modern Christians should follow their conscience if it tells them the Church is wrong (e.g. on artificial contraception).
- The Bible often needs to be interpreted, the teachings of the Church come through the Pope, bishops, conferences, etc., but conscience is God speaking directly to individuals and so should be followed.

Why some Christians think they should not always follow their conscience

- People have heard the voice of God telling them to do bad things. If people can be mistaken about the voice of God, they could be mistaken about the voice of conscience.
- If Christians follow the teachings of the Bible they are doing what all Christians agree is the Christian thing to do.
- If Christians follow the teachings of the Church, they are doing what other Christians think is right.
- If everyone followed their conscience rather than laws, there would be chaos as no one would know what sort of behaviour to expect from each other (see Topic 4.1, page 61).

Key points

Conscience is the inner feeling that makes people think something is right or wrong. Many Christians think conscience is the way God speaks to Christians today and so is the main guide for making moral decisions. Other Christians think it is safer to follow the Bible or the Church.

Evaluation questions

You may be required to argue for and against following your conscience as the best way to make moral decisions.

1. To argue for, you should use the reasons above left for why some Christians believe they should follow their conscience.

2. To argue against, you should use the reasons on the left for why some Christians think they should not always follow their conscience.

Topic 1.4 Situation Ethics as a guide for making moral decisions

Key points

Situation Ethics is the idea that the only moral rule Christians need is to love your neighbour. Christians who follow this believe that all they need to do when faced with a moral decision is work out what is the most loving thing to do in that situation. Other Christians think this can cause problems because you never know all the facts or all the consequences of your actions.

Evaluation questions

You may be required to argue for and against Christians basing their moral decisions on Situation Ethics.

1. To argue for, you should use the reasons on the right for why some Christians use Situation Ethics as a guide for making moral decisions.

2. To argue against, you should use the reasons below for why some Christians think Situation Ethics is wrong.

Main points

What is Situation Ethics?

Many of those Christians who believe that conscience is more important than the Bible or the Church believe that Christians should follow **Situation Ethics** which began with an American Christian thinker, Joseph Fletcher. He taught that following the rules of the Bible or the Church is wrong for Christians because Jesus taught that love is the most important thing and so Christians should only follow the Bible and/or the Church if what they say is the most loving thing to do.

For example, the Bible says that stealing is wrong, so it would be wrong to steal nuclear weapons from a madman. But Situation Ethics would say a Christian should steal the nuclear weapons because that would be the most loving thing for society. In the same way, the Church would say that a twelve-year-old girl made pregnant by a rape attack could not have an abortion because abortion is wrong, but Situation Ethics would allow her to have an abortion because it would be the most loving thing.

Why some Christians use Situation Ethics as a guide for making moral decisions

- Jesus seemed to follow Situation Ethics because he over-ruled what the Old Testament said when he thought it was unloving. For example, healing people on the Sabbath because he said it was more important to do good than to obey the Sabbath laws.
- They think Christians should only do what will produce good results, such as stealing the nuclear weapons and allowing the twelve-year-old to have an abortion.
- Jesus said the greatest commandments are to love God and love your neighbour, meaning Christians should always do what will have the most loving results.
- They believe that Christianity is a religion of love and so Christians should make their moral decisions based on love not laws.

Why some Christians think Situation Ethics is wrong

- They believe the Bible is God's word to Christians about how to live, so it should be the basis for moral decision-making.
- They believe they should follow the Ten Commandments and the Sermon on the Mount rather than relying on their own ideas.
- They think the Church knows better what Christians should do than an individual Christian.
- They claim you can never be sure of the consequences of a choice because you can never know you have all the facts of the situation. Therefore it is better to follow the rules of the Church and/or Bible.

Topic 1.5 Why some Christians use a variety of authorities in making moral decisions

Main points

Although some Christians would use only one authority when making a moral decision, other Christians might use more than one.

- Protestants might usually use the Bible as their authority because it is straightforward to use, for example, do not steal, do not murder. However, it is more difficult for modern issues such as contraception or civil partnerships. The Bible says nothing about contraception or civil partnerships, so they would have to look to the teaching of the Church or their conscience for guidance.
- Catholics would normally follow the authority of the Church, as the Magisterium applies the teachings of the Bible and the apostles to modern life. However, they might feel unable to apply the Church's ban on artificial contraceptives to the issue of supplying condoms to African states with lots of AIDS, and follow their conscience or Situation Ethics instead. In the same way they might use conscience or Situation Ethics to make a decision about civil partnerships as the Church says it is not wrong to be homosexual, but it is wrong to have homosexual sex.
- A Christian who usually followed their conscience might turn to the authority of the Bible or the Church if what their conscience was telling them went against what they knew was accepted Christian teaching. A good example would be if a Christian heard the voice of God telling them to kill all doctors who perform abortions. The Bible and the Church say that it is wrong to murder whatever the reasons. So they would use the authority of the Bible or the Church to reject the voice of their conscience because, although they might feel the purpose of stopping abortions may be a good one, that does not justify killing people to achieve it.
- A Christian who usually used Situation Ethics might decide that the issue was so complicated and the effects of a choice so uncertain that the safest thing would be to follow either the authority of the Bible or the authority of the Church because they are more likely to give the right choice than an individual trying to work it all out for themselves.

Key points

When Christians have to decide what to do about an issue they can:

- use what the Bible says about it
- use what Church leaders say about it
- use what they feel is right (their conscience)
- work out what is the most loving thing to do (Situation Ethics).

Most Christians would use more than one of these.

Evaluation questions

You are unlikely to be asked an evaluation question on this topic, but you could use:

- the first bullet in answering evaluation questions on the Bible
- the second bullet in answering evaluation questions on the teachings of the Church
- the third bullet in answering evaluation questions on conscience
- the fourth bullet in answering evaluation questions on Situation Ethics.

Topic 1.6 Human rights in the United Kingdom

Key points

Citizens of the UK have certain basic rights such as the right to life, the right to liberty, the right to a fair trial, the right to freedom of conscience and religion, the right to marry and start a family, the right to an education, the right to take part in free elections. These rights are meant to make sure that all UK citizens are treated fairly and equally by the state.

Main points

In 1998, the Human Rights Act was passed giving UK citizens the rights given to EU citizens in the European Union Charter of Fundamental Rights.

Your main **human rights** are:
- The right to life – this means that the law must protect you from being killed.
- Freedom from torture and degraded treatment.
- Freedom from slavery and forced labour.
- The right to liberty – this means that people are free to do anything that is not against the law and can only be detained according to the law.
- The right to a fair trial.
- The right to respect for private and family life – no one has the right to enter your home without the law's permission and no one has the right to publish information about your private life unless it can be shown to be 'in the public interest'.
- Freedom of thought, conscience and religion – no one can be persecuted for their ideas and beliefs.
- Freedom of expression – this means people can say what they think and publish their ideas, but only as long as they do not break other laws.
- The right to meet with others to discuss their views and to organise public demonstrations to publicise their views.
- The right to marry or form a civil partnership and start a family.
- The right to own property.
- The right to an education.
- The right to take part in free elections – this includes the right to vote, the right to stand as a candidate and the right to a secret ballot.

If any of these rights and freedoms are abused you have a right to go to court even if the abuse was by someone like a police officer. Clearly, having such rights gives all citizens of the UK a duty to respect the rights of other people.

Evaluation questions

You may be required to argue for and against human rights being important.

1. To argue for, you could use such reasons as:
   - Without human rights such as the right to liberty and a fair trial, you could find yourself living in a dictatorship because all opposition leaders have been imprisoned.
   - Without the right to freedom of thought and freedom of expression, minority religions and minority political parties could be banned.
   - Without the right to take part in free elections, there would be no democracy.

2. To argue against, you could use such reasons as:
   - People abuse human rights laws, for example prisoners claiming that their punishment infringes their human rights.
   - In a democracy you don't need special human rights because people can vote for what they want.
   - You ought to be able to torture terrorists to find out where they have planted bombs as this will save innocent lives.

Topic 1.7 Why human rights are important for Christians

Main points

Importance of human rights

Christians believe that human rights are important because:

- The right to life is a basic Christian belief because of the belief that life is holy and belongs to God (sanctity of life).
- Christians believe that all people are made in the image of God and so are one human family. Therefore it is important to Christians that everyone is treated fairly and equally and so people need human rights laws to protect minorities.
- Freedom of thought, conscience and religion, freedom of expression, freedom of assembly and association are an essential part of being Christian. Christians must have the legal right to believe in Christianity, to share their beliefs with others, to meet together for worship and to have processions to celebrate Easter and Pentecost.
- It is also an essential human right for Christians not to be disadvantaged compared to others, since it means that employers cannot discriminate against Christians over jobs and pay. For example, employers cannot refuse to employ Christians because they don't want religious people in the workplace.

Why some human rights can cause problems for Christians

Some Christians do not approve of all human rights because:

- Many Christians are against the right to form civil partnerships because they believe that homosexuality is against God's will as shown in the Bible.
- Some Christians are against the right to marry a person from a different faith. They believe that Christians should only marry Christians so that the children are brought up as Christians.
- Some Christians are against the right of homosexuals to raise a family. They believe that children should be brought up by a mother and a father.
- There might also be problems for the Catholic Church if human rights laws were used to argue for the right for women to become priests, or the right of priests to marry.

Key points

All human rights are important to Christians because they believe that all people are made in the image of God and so should have the same rights. They are also important because Christians believe in the sanctity of life and so all life belongs to God. However, some rights can cause problems for Christians, for example when homosexuals and women want to have equal rights in religion.

Evaluation questions

You may be required to argue for and against human rights being important for Christians.

1. To argue for, you could use the reasons above left for Christians believing human rights are important.

2. To argue against, you could use the reasons on the left for why human rights can cause problems for Christians.

Topic 1.8 Why it is important to take part in democratic and electoral processes

Key points

It is important for people to vote in elections and be involved in politics because it gives people a chance to choose and affect governments and councils. These can have a big influence because they set taxes, pass new laws and run organisations like the NHS, and people should have a say in how this is done.

Evaluation questions

You may be required to argue for and against it being important to take part in electoral processes (vote in elections/join or form a political party/stand as a candidate in elections).

1. To argue for, you could use the reasons on the right for why it is important.

2. People who argue against are likely to use such reasons as:
   - One vote makes no difference to the outcome as there are over 60 million people in the UK.
   - All politicians are sleazebags who are not worth voting for.
   - It doesn't matter who is voted in, they will just have to do what the EU says.

Main points

What are electoral and democratic processes?

The UK is a democracy. This means that every UK citizen over the age of eighteen is entitled to vote for:

- MPs (the government must have a majority of the MPs in the House of Commons)
- local councillors
- MEPs (members of the European Parliament).

Every UK citizen over the age of eighteen is entitled to be a candidate in any of these elections as long as they can find ten electors to nominate them and put down a financial deposit.

Every citizen has the right to try to change the policies of the government, local council or EU by:

- joining or forming a political party
- joining or forming a pressure group
- having a meeting with their MP, councillor or MEP.

Why is it important to take part in electoral and democratic processes?

- You pay income tax on your wages and VAT on what you buy, and voting gives you some control over how much this is.
- Local councils set the level of the council tax you have to pay, so voting gives you some control over how much this is.
- The European Parliament has some control over EU spending, so it is important to vote in European elections.
- Taking part in electoral processes and democratic processes gives you a chance to affect new laws which may be passed.
- The national government is responsible for important things like the armed forces, schools, the NHS, benefits and pensions. Voting gives you a say in how these are run.
- Local councils are responsible for such things as: refuse disposal, leisure and cultural services, trading standards, social services, housing services, maintaining the roads, etc. These are important areas that you need to have a say in.
- Your ancestors fought to have these electoral and democratic rights and so you should use them.
- If people in the UK do not use their rights, a small number of people could elect a government which took away our rights so that they could treat us badly.

Topic 1.9 Christian teachings on moral duties and responsibilities

Main points

Most Christians believe that they should take part in electoral and democratic processes, but that they should be guided by Christian teachings such as:

1 The Golden Rule

Jesus said that the Golden Rule is: 'So in everything, do to others what you would have them do to you, for this sums up the Law and the Prophets' (Matthew 7:12).

Christians must use the Golden Rule when voting. For example, if a party wanted to send all asylum seekers back to their home country, a Christian would have to think, 'If I were a member of an ethnic group being slaughtered by the army, would I want to be sent back to be slaughtered?'

2 The Parable of the Sheep and the Goats

'At the end of the world, the Son of Man will judge everyone. Like a shepherd, he will separate the sheep from goats. The sheep will be those who fed Jesus when he was hungry, gave him drink when he was thirsty, took him in when he was a stranger, clothed him when he needed clothes, looked after him when he was sick, visited him when he was in prison and they will go to heaven. However, the goats will be told that as they did not do any of these things for other people, they will go to hell.' (Adapted from Matthew 25:31–46.)

This parable shows it is the duty of Christians to help the poor and suffering by taking part in politics. For example, if a party's policy was to cut off benefits to the jobless who refused jobs, a Christian might accept this because they would not refuse work if they were jobless, but they would also have to think about the effects of the policy on the children of the jobless.

3 Am I my brother's keeper?

In Genesis 4, Adam's son Cain is jealous of his brother Abel and murders him. When God asks Cain where his brother is, Cain replies, 'I don't know. Am I my brother's keeper?' God then punishes Cain showing that God created humans to be their brothers' keepers, that is to look after each other.

This is explained more fully by St John who says: 'We should love one another. Do not be like Cain who … murdered his brother … If anyone had material possessions and sees his brother in need but has no pity on him, how can the love of God be in him?' (1 John 3:11–18).

These Christian teachings on being our brother's keeper show Christians that they have a duty to look after everyone in need.

Key points

Most Christians believe that they should take part in electoral and democratic processes to make society more Christian. They are guided by Christian teachings such as:

- the Golden Rule, which says Christians should treat other people in the way they would like to be treated
- the Parable of the Sheep and the Goats, which says that Christians should help the homeless, the sick and the hungry
- the story of Cain and Abel, which tells Christians that they are responsible for the rights of others.

Evaluation questions

You may be required to argue for and against it being important for Christians to be guided by Christian teachings when taking part in democratic and electoral processes.

1. To argue for, you could use the points 1–3 on the left.
2. People who argue against are likely to use such reasons as:
- Christians don't need to take part in electoral processes because Jesus said that loving God is the greatest commandment, so it is more important to love God than take part in electoral processes.
- Going to Mass every Sunday is more important than taking part in electoral processes.
- Christianity is about loving God, elections are about politics and the two should not mix.

Topic 1.10 The nature of genetic engineering, including cloning

Key points

Genetic engineering is finding out which genes cause diseases, such as muscular dystrophy, and then working out how the genes can be changed (often by cloning) so that the disease does not develop. Genetic research in the UK is controlled by the law and by the Human Fertilisation and Embryology Authority. Some people are in favour because it can lead to cures for dreadful diseases, some people are against because they think the likely effects are not really known.

Evaluation questions

Evaluation questions are dealt with in Topic 1.11 (page 15) as you will be asked to refer to Christianity in your answer.

Main points

Genetic engineering in medical issues is using techniques of gene development to find cures or prevention for disease and disabilities in humans. Scientists are involved in genetic research into: cystic fibrosis, muscular dystrophy, sickle-cell anaemia, Tay–Sachs disease and Huntington's chorea.

Most genetic research has been based on:
- germline gene therapy, which allows cells that transmit information from one generation to the next to be changed
- pre-implantation genetic diagnosis (PGD), which removes defective genes from embryos.

Stem cell research

More recently, cloning processes have been used to grow healthy cells to replace the diseased ones. This process involves creating stem cells either from embryos produced for in-vitro fertilisation (IVF) but not used, or from adult bone marrow or blood. Stem cell research has been legal in the UK since 2001.

Non-religious arguments in favour of genetic engineering

- It offers the prospect of cures for currently incurable diseases.
- It is being done in other countries and so is available to those rich enough to travel and pay for treatments.
- Cloning using animal eggs, as in cybrids (a human nucleus in an empty animal egg), does not involve any loss of human life.
- Genetic research is closely monitored by the law, but has vast potential benefits.

Non-religious arguments against genetic engineering

- There is too little information about the long-term consequences.
- It has effects which can't be changed, so if anything went wrong it would be permanent.
- It places too much power in the hands of scientists who could produce scientifically created human beings.
- It treats the human body as no different from plants.

Topic 1.11 Different attitudes to genetic engineering and cloning in Christianity

Main points

There are several attitudes to genetic engineering among Christians:

Liberal Protestants support genetic engineering because:

- Jesus showed that Christians should do all they can to cure disease.
- Finding genetic cures is no different from finding drug cures.
- There is a difference between creating cells and creating people.
- Embryos are not foetuses until they are fourteen days old.
- They accept the non-religious arguments in favour of genetic engineering (see Topic 1.10, page 14).

Roman Catholics, and some other Christians, agree with genetic research as long as it does not involve the use of embryos because:

- Life begins at the moment of conception whether in a womb or a test tube and killing life is wrong.
- Killing an embryo is killing human life.
- Embryos have been produced by un-Christian means (see Topic 2.7, page 31).

Some Christians are against all genetic research because:

- They believe that God creates the genetic make-up of each person at conception and people have no right to interfere with this.
- It is trying to play God which is a great sin.
- It is wrong to try to make Earth perfect; only heaven is perfect.

Key points

- Some Christians allow all genetic research, as long as it is to find cures for diseases, because Jesus was a healer.
- Some Christians allow genetic research which does not involve the destruction of embryos, which they believe to be human life.
- Some Christians oppose all genetic research because they believe it is 'playing God'.

Evaluation questions

You may be required to argue for and against genetic research.

1. To argue for, you should use the reasons why some Christians agree with genetic research, given above left.

2. To argue against, you could use either the reasons against given on the left or the arguments against in Topic 1.10 (page 14).

How to answer questions on Section 1

The a) question – key words

These questions give you up to two marks just for knowing the key words and their meanings. This means you must learn the key words because you can gain ten per cent of the marks if you get the a) questions right.

Have a look at the following examples.

Question
What is the Decalogue?   (2 marks)

Up to four marks will be awarded for your spelling, punctuation and grammar in your answer to Section 1 of the exam paper. This means you should take extra care with your spelling and make sure you use full stops and capital letters. You should use paragraphs if your answers to parts c) and/or d) are long.

Four marks for spelling, punctuation and grammar can move an A to an A*, a B to an A, etc., remember to take extra care with your spelling and punctuation in your answers to Section 1.

Answer

The Ten Commandments.

> Two marks for a correct definition.

Question
What is the Church?   (2 marks)

Answer

The community of Christians.

> Two marks for a correct definition.

The b) question – what do you think?

These questions give you up to four marks for giving your own opinion about one of the issues, but you will only gain marks if you give reasons for your opinion!

You must decide what you think about the issues and ideas you study. The questions are meant to be quite easy and to get full marks you just need to give two developed reasons. They are really like part (i) of an evaluation question (question d) where you have to give two reasons. So, to answer a response question, you could use two of the reasons from the point of view you agree with in the evaluation question advice for each topic.

The following example shows you what is meant by developed reasons.

Question
Do you think human rights laws are important? Give TWO reasons for your point of view. (4 marks)

Answer

Yes I do think they are important because without human rights such as the right to liberty and a fair trial, you could find your self living in a dictatorship ...

> One mark for a reason.

... because all opposition leaders could be imprisoned.

> Two marks because the reason is developed.

Also, without the right to freedom of thought and freedom of expression, minority religions could be banned ...

> Three marks for a second reason.

... and minority political parties could be banned.

> Four marks because the reason is developed.

> Total = four marks.

The c) question – explain

You can gain two marks for giving a brief reason in basic English even if the spelling and grammar are poor. You will also only get two marks if you describe the issue rather than trying to explain it.

You can gain four marks by giving two brief reasons with a limited command of English and little use of specialist vocabulary.

You can gain five marks by giving three brief reasons, but this will rise to six marks if it is written in a clear style of English with some use of specialist vocabulary.

You can gain seven marks by using four brief reasons, but this will rise to eight marks if you write in a clear and correct style of English with a correct use of specialist vocabulary where appropriate.

Explain questions are where your Quality of Written Communication is tested, so you should answer these questions in a formal style of English, be careful with your spelling and try to use some specialist vocabulary. You can gain four extra marks on the paper if your written English is good, which could move an A to an A*, a B to an A, etc.

Have a look at the following example.

Question

Explain why some Christians allow genetic engineering, but some do not. (8 marks)

Answer

Some Christians allow genetic engineering because Jesus showed that Christians should do all they can to cure disease.

They also believe that finding genetic cures is no different from finding drug cures and so there is no reason for not allowing it.

Some Christians do not allow genetic engineering because they believe that God creates the genetic make-up of each person at conception and people have no right to interfere with this.

These Christians also feel that using genetic engineering is trying to play God. This is putting yourself on a par with God which is a great sin banned by the Bible and the Church.

> LEVEL 1: two marks for giving a reason for an attitude expressed in basic English.

> LEVEL 2: by giving a second reason for the attitude, the answer goes up to level 2 and because the answer is written in clear English it would gain four marks.

> LEVEL 3: by giving a reason for a different attitude, the answer moves up to level 3 and because the answer is written in a clear style of English with some use of specialist vocabulary (Jesus, genetic cures, creates, genetic make-up, conception) it would gain six marks.

> LEVEL 4: by adding a further reason for the second attitude, the answer moves up to level 4 and because it is written in a clear and correct style of English with extra specialist vocabulary (play God, on a par with God, sin, Bible, Church) it would gain eight marks – full marks.

The d) question – evaluation

To answer these questions, you need to decide what you think about the quotation and then give three reasons for why you think that.

Then you need to give three reasons why some people (for example, Christians if you are an atheists, or atheists if you are a Christian) would disagree with you.

One of your points of view should always be religious so that you can give religious reasons.

Have a look at the following example.

Question

'You need more guidance than the Bible when you make a moral decision.'

(i) Do you agree? Give reasons for your opinion.   (3 marks)
(ii) Give reasons why some people may disagree with you.   (3 marks)

Answer

One mark for a personal opinion with a reason.	(i) *I agree because the Bible says nothing about modern issues like contraception or civil partnerships.*
Another reason is given so it moves up to two marks.	*Also, some Christians believe they need the Church to explain what the Bible means for today.*
The answer now gives another reason for their opinion, so it moves up to three marks.	*Finally, some Christians believe that the Bible was written by humans inspired by God, so many of its attitudes need to be altered because of the* **social changes** *in the modern world (for example, St Paul's attitude to women and slaves).*
One mark for a reason why some people might disagree.	(ii) *I can see why some Christians would disagree with me because they believe that the Bible is the word of God and so is God's guidance to humans about how to make decisions.*
Another reason is given, so it moves up to two marks.	*They believe they only need the Bible because it contains God's teachings on how Christians should behave. The Decalogue, for example, gives very clear guidance on such things as: the treatment of parents, stealing, murder, adultery, lying, etc.*
The answer now gives another reason for some people disagreeing, so it moves up to three marks.	*They also believe that as the Bible contains the teachings of Jesus on how to live, and as Christians believe Jesus is the Son of God, his teachings about moral decision-making can never go out of date.*
This answer to question d) can gain full marks because both parts refer to Christianity.	

SECTION 1 TEST

SECTION 1: Rights and responsibilities

Answer both questions

1. a) What is the Golden Rule? (2 marks)

   b) Do you think you are your brother's keeper? Give two reasons for your point of view. (4 marks)

   c) Explain why some Christians use Situation Ethics as a guide for making moral decisions. (8 marks)

   d) 'No Christian should use genetic engineering.'
      (i) Do you agree? Give reasons for your opinion. (3 marks)
      (ii) Give reasons why some people may disagree with you. (3 marks)

   In your answer you should refer to Christianity.

   (Total: 20 marks)

2. a) What is social change? (2 marks)

   b) Do you think the teachings of the Church are important for making moral decisions? Give two reasons for your point of view. (4 marks)

   c) Explain why human rights are important for Christians. (8 marks)

   d) 'It doesn't matter whether or not you vote.'
      (i) Do you agree? Give reasons for your opinion. (3 marks)
      (ii) Give reasons why some people may disagree with you. (3 marks)

   (Total: 20 marks)

You should now use the mark scheme in the Appendix, page 83 to mark your answers, and the self-help tables in the Appendix, pages 84–85 to see how you can improve your performance. If you need more help with the mark scheme for these questions, go to www.hoddereducation.co.uk/religionandsociety

Section 2 Environmental and medical issues

KEY WORDS FOR SECTION 2

Artificial insemination	injecting semen into the uterus by artificial means
Conservation	protecting and preserving natural resources and the environment
Creation	the act of creating the universe or the universe which has been created
Embryo	a fertilised egg in the first eight weeks after conception
Environment	the surroundings in which plants and animals live and on which they depend to live
Global warming	the increase in the temperature of the Earth's atmosphere (thought to be caused by the greenhouse effect)
Infertility	not being able to have children
In-vitro fertilisation	the method of fertilising a human egg in a test-tube
Natural resources	naturally occurring materials, such as oil and fertile land, which can be used by humans
Organ donation	giving organs to be used in transplant surgery
Stewardship	looking after something so it can be passed on to the next generation
Surrogacy	an arrangement whereby a woman bears a child on behalf of another woman

Topic 2.1 Global warming

Main points

Global warming means that the Earth is warmer than it has been for over 1000 years which could lead to some coastal areas disappearing, and countries such as Spain becoming deserts.

The causes of global warming

1 The greenhouse effect

Most scientists believe that global warming is caused by human activity in what is known as the greenhouse effect. The burning of fossil fuels (gas, coal and oil) produces carbon dioxide (our carbon footprint). This produces a barrier in the atmosphere rather like the glass in a greenhouse so that the heat from the sun can get through, but cannot get back out again, so causing the Earth's temperature to rise. Humans are now producing far more carbon emissions, therefore the Earth's temperature is rising.

2 Natural climate change

Some scientists claim it is a result of natural changes because the warmest periods in the last 10,000 years happened well before humans started to produce carbon footprints. They say that if the greenhouse effect were true, the troposphere (the top layer of the atmosphere) should be heating up faster than the Earth's surface, but it does not seem to be.

3 Solar activity

Some scientists claim that changes in the Earth's temperature are caused by the amount of radiation coming from the sun. When solar activity is high, fewer clouds form so more of the sun's heat reaches the Earth and it warms up.

Possible solutions

- Using ways of making electricity which do not produce carbon dioxide: wind power, sea power, hydroelectric power and solar power. In June 2008, the UK government announced that by 2050 there will be no carbon emissions from Britain's power stations.
- Car manufacturers are using ethanol, biodiesel, electric batteries and hydrogen to power cars without carbon emissions. However, biofuels (ethanol and biodiesel) are produced from crops which could be used for food, and electric batteries rely on electricity produced by power stations using oil or coal.
- It is also possible to improve the efficiency and reduce the pollution caused by such things as cars. By 2010 the total tonnage of pollutants emitted by cars will reduce by 75 per cent compared with 1992, even though the number of cars on the road will increase.
- Increased use of public transport (trains are by far the lowest carbon emission form of transport) could greatly reduce carbon emissions.

Key points

Global warming means that the atmosphere of the Earth is getting warmer and this could mean that some towns and cities near the sea could disappear under water.

Most scientists think global warming is caused by people putting too much carbon into the atmosphere, but some think it is caused by activity on the sun or by the nature of Earth's climate.

Most scientists think global warming could be solved by reducing carbon emissions by using other ways of producing electricity, such as wind, water, waves, etc., and by running cars on fuels which do not emit carbon.

Evaluation questions

You may be required to argue for and against carbon emissions being the main cause of global warming.

1. To argue for, you could use the points on the greenhouse effect above left.

2. To argue against, you could use the points on natural climate change and solar activity above left.

Topic 2.2 Forms of pollution and their possible solutions

Key points

Pollution takes several forms. Acid rain is caused by high-level carbon emissions (as global warming could be) and damages buildings. Human waste (refuse and sewage) can cause major health problems if not dealt with properly as can radioactive waste from nuclear power plants. Eutrophication caused by nitrates and sewage kills fish in streams and rivers, and litter dropped by humans leads to an increase in rats.

Possible solutions are:

- producing electricity by wind, water, etc.
- more efficient means of waste disposal, recycling, nuclear reprocessing and geological storage
- people being made to stop dropping litter.

Main points

The main forms of pollution other than carbon emissions are listed below.

1 Acid rain

Buildings and forests in countries such as Sweden and Germany are being destroyed by the acid rain coming from the UK. This is caused by the burning of fossil fuels which change the pH of the rainwater in clouds making it so acidic that it can burn things when it comes to Earth.

2 Human waste

The waste produced by humans in the form of sewage, refuse (rubbish put into bins) and litter (rubbish left on the streets, etc.) is a major threat to the future of the planet. As the world economy grows so does its production of wastes – Europe produces more than 2.5 billion tonnes of solid waste a year. Human excreta and other waterborne waste products are transported through sewers to sewage works for treatment, but untreated sewage causes water pollution and eutrophication.

Compost bins and litter have led the rat population in the UK to grow to 70 million. Rats bring many diseases to humans such as the deadly Weil's disease. Litter also causes thousands of bike and car accidents when it is on roads, and it is estimated that a fire breaks out every twelve minutes because of litter.

3 Eutrophication

This is the lack of oxygen in rivers killing fish and making water plants grow. It is caused by:

- fertilisers being washed into streams
- sewage pollution
- a lack of trees to soak up nitrogen.

This could lead to major health problems for humans, such as septicaemia.

4 Radioactive pollution

Nuclear power stations are carbon free, but produce nuclear waste which will take thousands if not millions of years to be safe. When humans come into contact with nuclear waste, they can be killed, get cancer and have genetically mutated children.

Possible solutions

- The solution to acid rain is to create electricity from wind, sun, tides and nuclear energy.
- The problems of waste could be solved by a combination of recycling, using incinerators to produce electricity, and sewage to produce methane gas. But each method has problems, e.g. reusing glass bottles can need more energy to sterilise them than to make new ones.
- The problem of litter would be solved if people stopped dropping litter! The UK has laws to make this happen – those who leave litter can be given an on-the-spot fine and badly littered areas reported to the local council must be cleared within a fixed period.
- Better sewage treatment, fewer phosphates in detergents and fewer nitrates in farm fertilisers could stop eutrophication. However, organic farming uses manure causing an increase of nitrates in streams and rivers.
- Some nuclear waste can be reprocessed (Sellafield plant in Cumbria is one of only two in the world) so that 97 per cent of the waste can be re-used. However, the remaining three per cent of waste has to be stored. The UK government is working on a project to isolate the waste deep inside a suitable rock formation to ensure that no radioactivity can ever reach the surface.

Remember: carbon emissions are also a form of pollution.

Evaluation questions

You may be required to argue for and against the problems of pollution being able to be solved.

1. To argue for, you could use the possible solutions on the left and the possible solutions to global warming in Topic 2.1 (page 21), as carbon emissions are a form of pollution.

2. To argue against, you could use such reasons as:
   - Carbon emissions are set to double between 2010 and 2050 so any action is only likely to limit the rise.
   - Recycling is not working as the costs of recycling are so high.
   - Nuclear waste is going to be a problem for thousands of years as it does not decay.

Topic 2.3 The scarcity of natural resources

Key points

Resources are a problem because those which cannot be grown again (non-renewable resources), such as oil, natural gas and metals, will disappear. This will lead to major problems in our lifestyles.

However, alternative energy supplies, recycling and changing lifestyles could help solve the problems.

Evaluation questions

You may be required to argue for and against the problem of resources being solvable.

1. To argue for, you could use the points from possible solutions below right.

2. To argue against, you could use such reasons as:
   - Renewable resources for producing electricity are very expensive and will not work for many countries.
   - Using plants for plastics and bio-diesel is going to reduce the food supply and people need food.
   - Recycling is very expensive and uses a lot of electricity.

Main points

Natural resources are naturally occurring materials, such as oil and fertile land, which can be used by humans.

They can be divided into two types:

1. *Renewable resources*. These are resources which humans can use over and over again such as: wind power, solar power, water power, and fertile land producing food and biofuels. Using renewable resources causes no problems but using them to produce electricity is often more expensive.

2. *Finite or non-renewable resources*. These are resources which disappear once they are used such as: oil, coal, iron, tin, copper, uranium, natural gas.

Human use of finite resources causes major problems

- The problem is most obvious in the case of oil. It is not only petrol and diesel that come from oil. All plastics and road surfaces, most candles, polishes and chemical foodstuffs come from oil. Clearly, if the oil begins to dry up, there will be major effects.
- Metals cause similar problems. Everything from car panels to kitchen appliances comes from finite ores such as iron, aluminium and tin. Many scientists feel that unless we stop using these resources as we are, they will soon run out, giving us a problem as bad as the problems of global warming and pollution.

Possible solutions

- We could use renewable resources to make electricity: nuclear power, wind power, sea power, hydroelectric power and solar power.
- Car manufacturers are looking at water, sugar cane and electric batteries as ways of powering cars.
- Recycling will enable the lifetime of many finite resources to be extended. For example, some cars are now made of almost 75 per cent recycled materials.
- Scientists are working on using chemicals from plants to produce plastics.
- Some people think an alternative lifestyle is necessary and they only use natural products (e.g. cotton or wool clothes) and ride bikes instead of owning a car.

Topic 2.4 Christian teachings on stewardship

Main points

Christians believe that God gave humans the **stewardship** (looking after something so that it can be passed on to the next generation) of the Earth and its resources. The Bible teaches that Christians:

- were given the right to rule over the Earth, but only as his stewards (Genesis)
- must treat animals and the land kindly (every fifty years they should not grow crops)
- have a responsibility to leave the Earth a better place than they found it (Jesus' teaching in the Parable of the Talents/Minas)
- have a responsibility to make sure the Earth's resources are shared fairly (Jesus' teaching in the Gospels)
- will be judged on whether they have been good stewards of God's Earth (Jesus' teaching in the Gospels).

How beliefs about stewardship affect Christian attitudes to the environment

- The responsibility to be God's stewards and to leave the Earth a better place than they found it means that Christians should try to reduce pollution and preserve resources.
- Christians should show stewardship by working to share the Earth's resources more fairly and improve the standard of living in LEDCs (less economically developed countries).
- The belief that they will be judged on their behaviour as stewards means Christians should help the work of groups which try to reduce pollution and **conserve** resources.
- Christians should judge what they do in their life by the standards of Christian stewardship. It is only by being a good steward and conserving the **environment** that a Christian can become a good Christian.

However, Christians believe human interests come first, for example shutting down a factory which causes pollution but employs three thousand people would not be a Christian solution.

Key points

Christians believe that God made humans to look after the world as his stewards – to have authority over animals and plants. However, the Bible also teaches that Christians should care for the environment and leave the Earth a better place than they found it.

Evaluation questions

You may be required to argue for and against following religious teachings on stewardship being the best way to solve the problems of the environment.

1. To argue for, you could use the points on the left on how beliefs about stewardship affect Christian attitudes to the environment.

2. To argue against, you could use such reasons as:
   - Only government action can deal with problems like the disposal of waste.
   - Religion might change people's attitudes, but it won't build alternative energy producers such as wind farms.
   - Recycling has to be organised on an international basis which would be difficult to do by religion.

Topic 2.5.1 The teachings of Islam on stewardship

As you only need to study one religion, you should only learn one of the four topics on pages 26–29 – the religion you have studied at school.

Key points

Islam teaches that God created humans as his stewards of the Earth. He showed people how to look after the Earth in the Qur'an. Life is a test and God will judge Muslims on how well they have looked after the world.

Evaluation questions

Evaluation questions will only ask you to refer to one religion, so you would be best just to use Christianity in answering evaluation questions, although you could use extra reasons from Islam.

Main points

- Islam teaches that God created Adam as his Khalifah (vice-regent or vice-gerent – someone who looks after things for you). This means that all Muslims are God's khalifahs who have to keep the balance of **creation** and look after the Earth for God in the way set out in the Qur'an and the Shari'ah.
- Islam also teaches that people will be judged by God on the way they have looked after the Earth and the life on Earth.
- Islam teaches that this life is a test from God. A main part of the test is looking after the environment in the way of Islam. Those who fail the test will be punished.

How Islamic teachings about stewardship affect attitudes to the environment

- The responsibility to be God's khalifah means that Muslims should try to reduce pollution and preserve resources.
- The Shari'ah and ummah tell Muslims that stewardship includes sharing the Earth's resources, so Muslims should work to share the Earth's resources more fairly and improve the standard of living in LEDCs.
- The belief that they will be judged on their behaviour as khalifahs means Muslims have a duty to help the work of groups which try to reduce pollution and conserve resources.
- There is a unity and balance in creation, therefore Muslims have a duty to preserve the environment.

However, Muslims believe that human interests come first and so the effects of environmental projects on humans cannot be ignored.

Topic 2.5.2 The teachings of Judaism on stewardship

Main points

Judaism teaches that God made humans as stewards of his Earth and gave them control of the Earth and all its creatures. However, as God's stewards, Jews must look after the Earth in the way God showed in these mitzvot:

- Around every town there must be an area of open parkland.
- At the festival of New Year for Trees, trees should be planted where they are needed.
- Every fifty years no crops should be planted nor fruit harvested, so nature can recharge its batteries.

How Jewish teachings about stewardship affect attitudes to the environment

- The responsibility to be God's stewards and to leave the Earth a better place than they found it means that Jews should try to reduce pollution and preserve resources.
- Jews should show stewardship by working to share the Earth's resources more fairly and improve the standard of living in LEDCs.
- The belief that they will be judged on their behaviour as stewards means Jews should help the work of groups which try to reduce pollution and conserve resources.
- God created the environment as something which is good, therefore Jews have a duty to preserve the environment.
- Orthodox Jews must obey the mitzvot so they must care for the environment.

However, Jews believe that human interests come first and so the effects of environmental projects on humans cannot be ignored.

As you only need to study one religion, you should only learn one of the four topics on pages 26–29 – the religion you have studied at school.

Key points

Judaism teaches that God created humans as his stewards of the Earth to have authority over animals and plants. He showed people how to look after the Earth in the mitzvot. Life is a test and God will judge Jews on how well they have looked after the world.

Evaluation questions

Evaluation questions will only ask you to refer to one religion, so you would be best just to use Christianity in answering evaluation questions, although you could use extra reasons from Judaism.

Topic 2.5.3 The teachings of Hinduism on stewardship

As you only need to study one religion, you should only learn one of the four topics on pages 26–29 – the religion you have studied at school.

Key points

Hindus believe they have a duty to show stewardship towards the Earth. The avatars of the gods as animals mean that Hindus should respect and look after animals. The law of nature and respect for life mean that Hindus should reduce pollution and try for a fair sharing of resources. However, some Hindus believe the interests of humans should come first.

Evaluation questions

Evaluation questions will only ask you to refer to one religion, so you would be best just to use Christianity in answering evaluation questions, although you could use extra reasons from Hinduism.

Main points

Although many Hindus would not talk about being stewards of the Earth, all Hindus believe they have certain duties towards the Earth. Hindu beliefs about stewardship include:

- Respect for animal life. The fact that many Hindu gods have appeared as animals, and that people may have been animals in previous lives, means animals must be respected and many Hindus are vegetarian.
- Respect for nature. Trees and nature are very special because the last stage of life is to live in the forest to find union with God.

How Hindu teachings about stewardship affect attitudes to the environment

- The need to respect the eternal law of nature means that Hindus should try to reduce pollution and preserve resources.
- The appearances of the gods as animals means many Hindus believe they should protect animals and be vegetarian.
- Hindus should show stewardship by working to share the Earth's resources more fairly and improve the standard of living in LEDCs.
- The belief in respect for life means Hindus should help the work of groups which try to reduce pollution and conserve resources.

Although Hindus should have a great respect for the environment, some Hindus feel that humans have the right to use the Earth's resources in any way they think is right. There is a lot of argument in India about industry and the environment.

Topic 2.5.4 The teachings of Sikhism on stewardship

Main points

Although Sikhs do not always talk about being stewards of the Earth, they believe they have a duty to look after the Earth because:

- The Guru Granth Sahib says that Sikhs should respect the light of God in the universe.
- The Guru Granth Sahib says that Sikhs should respect the light of God in people.
- The Guru Granth Sahib says that Sikhs should respect the light of God in life and nature.
- They must follow the examples of the Gurus who looked after the environment:
  - Baba Budha (a close friend of Guru Nanak who anointed the five Gurus after Nanak) made a place where tigers, goats, peacocks and snakes all existed in harmony amidst lakes and greenery.
  - When Guru Amar Das realised that the Beas River water was not fit for human consumption, he constructed a baoli, which provided safe drinking water for the people in an eco-friendly environment.
  - Guru Har Rai developed Kiratpur Sahib as a town of parks and gardens. He planted flowers and fruit-bearing trees all over the area, turning it into an idyllic place to live.

How Sikh teachings about stewardship affect attitudes to the environment

- Respecting the light of God in the universe means reducing pollution and preserving resources.
- Following the examples of the Gurus means Sikhs should protect animals and preserve eco-systems.
- Respecting God's light in people means Sikhs should try to share resources more fairly and improve the standard of living in LEDCs without causing more pollution.
- Respecting God's light in life and nature means Sikhs should share in and support the work of groups working to reduce pollution and conserve resources.

Although Sikhs should have a great respect for the environment, some Sikhs feel that in arguments between environmental protection and human jobs and living standards, the rights of humans should come first.

As you only need to study one religion, you should only learn one of the four topics on pages 26–29 – the religion you have studied at school.

Key points

Sikhs believe they have a duty to show stewardship towards the Earth. The examples of the Gurus mean that Sikhs should respect and look after animals. Respect for God's light in life and nature means that Sikhs should reduce pollution and try for a fair sharing of resources. However, most Sikhs believe the interests of humans should come first.

Evaluation questions

Evaluation questions will only ask you to refer to one religion, so you would be best just to use Christianity in answering evaluation questions, although you could use extra reasons from Sikhism.

Topic 2.6 The nature and importance of medical treatments for infertility

Key points

Infertility is when a couple cannot have a baby. There are now several medical treatments that can help infertile couples to have babies such as in-vitro fertilisation (IVF), artificial insemination and egg and embryo donation.

Infertility treatments are important because a lot of people in developed societies have fertility problems.

Evaluation questions

Questions on infertility treatments will ask you to refer to at least one religion, so the advice comes after Topic 2.7 (page 31).

Main points

The main medical treatments for **infertility** are:

- **In-vitro fertilisation** (IVF): an egg is taken from the mother's womb, fertilised in a test-tube and put back in the womb.
- **Artificial insemination** by husband (AIH): when the husband's sperm is put into the wife's womb by medical means.
- Artificial insemination by donor (AID): when an unknown man's sperm is put into the wife's womb by medical means.
- Egg donation: when an unknown woman's egg and the husband's sperm are fertilised by IVF and put back in the womb.
- **Embryo** donation: when both sperm and egg are from unknown donors and are fertilised by IVF then placed in the wife's womb.
- **Surrogacy**: when either the egg and sperm of husband and wife, or the egg or sperm of husband or wife and an unknown donor, are fertilised by IVF and then placed in another woman's womb and the baby handed to the husband and wife after the birth.

All the medical treatments now being used by couples in Britain are supervised by the Human Fertilisation and Embryology Authority (HFEA). Since 1 April 2005, children born from donated sperm, eggs or embryos have the right to discover their genetic parents when they are eighteen years old (about 50,000 children have been born from donations, but only about ten per cent of those have been told that they have other genetic parents).

Why infertility treatments are important

- Infertility has become much more of a problem. As many as 12.5 per cent of couples in the UK have fertility problems.
- According to the HFEA up to 1.5 million men in the UK alone have fertility problems.
- In 2007, twelve per cent of all births in the UK were as a result of fertility treatments.
- It is a part of human nature to want to have children and raise a family, and if treatments can help people achieve this, they must be important.
- Psychological problems are caused if couples are desperate to have children but cannot. Infertility treatments can prevent these problems from becoming mental illnesses.

Topic 2.7 Different attitudes to infertility treatments among Christians

Main points

There are two very different Christian views on infertility.

The Catholic view

Catholics believe that life is given by God and that no one has a right to children. The Catholic Church wants to help infertile couples, but only allows methods which do not affect the sanctity of life and in which sex acts are natural. Therefore all treatments involving medical technology are banned because:

- IVF involves fertilising several eggs, some of which are thrown away or used for experimentation. The Catholic Church believes that this is the same as abortion which the Church bans.
- All forms of artificial insemination or surrogacy involve the sin of male masturbation.
- All forms of embryo technology involve fertilisation being separated from sex, but God intended procreation to be a part of sex.

Other Christian Churches

The other Christian Churches allow IVF and AIH because:

- One of the purposes of Christian marriage is to have children, so infertility treatments must be good.
- In these treatments, the baby will be the biological offspring of its mother and father.
- The discarded embryos are not foetuses and so life is not being taken.

They do not ban other infertility treatments, but are worried because they involve problems of who the parent is and could lead to problems for the children as to who they are.

All Christians would encourage childless couples to adopt.

Key points

- Some Christians, mainly Catholics, do not allow any of the fertility treatments because they involve either immoral sex or taking the life of unwanted embryos.
- Other Christians allow IVF and AIH, but are suspicious of all other methods even though they do not ban them.

Evaluation questions

You may be required to argue for and against everyone having the right to have children.

1. To argue for, you could use the last two bullet points in why infertility treatments are important from Topic 2.6 (page 30) and the first bullet on the other Christian Churches and IVF and AIH on the left.

2. To argue against, you could use such reasons as:
   - Infertility may mean that God wants the person to do something other than raise a family.
   - Some treatments for infertility are against the teachings of religion.
   - Some treatments for infertility cause problems about who the parent is and could cause identity problems for the child.

Topic 2.8.1 Islam and infertility treatments

As you only need to study one religion, you should only learn one of the four topics on pages 32–33 – the religion you have studied at school.

Key points

Islam allows IVF and AIH because they only involve the husband and wife. Islam does not allow any other forms of fertility treatment because they cause problems concerning the identity of the parents.

Main points

Islam accepts IVF and AIH because:

- The egg and sperm are from the husband and wife.
- All Muslims should have a family.
- The unused embryos are not foetuses so life is not being taken.

Islam does not allow any other treatments because:

- They deny a child's right to know its natural parents.
- Egg or sperm donation is like adultery.
- They are the same as adoption which is banned in Islam.

Topic 2.8.2 Judaism and infertility treatments

Key points

All Jews accept IVF and AIH because having children is very important in Judaism. Some Jews accept all forms of fertility treatment, but some do not accept AID because of problems concerning the identity of parents.

Evaluation questions

Evaluation questions will only ask you to refer to one religion, so you would be best just to use Christianity in answering evaluation questions, although you could use extra reasons from the other religion you have studied.

Main points

IVF and AIH are accepted by all Jews because:

- Having children is very important in Judaism.
- The rabbis teach that humans can use the benefits of technology as long as they are within the mitzvot.
- The unused embryos are not foetuses so life is not being taken.

Orthodox Jews

- Most Orthodox Jews do not allow AID as it involves adultery.
- Surrogacy is not allowed as Jewishness is passed on by the mother.
- Many Orthodox Jews accept egg donation as long as it is donated by a Jewish woman.

Reform Jews

Most Reform Jews accept all treatments as they believe that upbringing makes a child Jewish.

Topic 2.8.3 Hinduism and infertility treatments

Main points

Many Hindus accept IVF, AIH, AID and egg donation because:

- All Hindus are expected to have a family and technology can be used to bring this about.
- The egg and sperm are from the husband and wife.
- The discarded embryos had no soul transferred to them.
- The Laws of Manu encourage infertile couples to adopt and so would have approved of infertility treatments.

Some Hindus do not allow AID, egg donation or surrogacy because:

- They believe caste is passed down through the parents.
- They believe that once an embryo has been created, it is alive and should not be killed.
- They see AID and egg donation as a form of adultery, which is banned by Hinduism.

> As you only need to study one religion, you should only learn one of the four topics on pages 32–33 – the religion you have studied at school.

Key points

- Many Hindus allow IVF, AIH, AID and egg donation because Hindus need to have a family.
- Some Hindus do not allow AID, egg donation or surrogacy because caste is passed on by the parents.

Topic 2.8.4 Sikhism and infertility treatments

Main points

Some Sikhs reject all infertility treatments involving technology because:

- They believe that once an embryo has been created, it is alive and should not be killed.
- They see AID and egg donation as a form of adultery, which is banned by Sikhism.

Many Sikhs accept AIH and IVF, but have worries about AID, egg donation and surrogacy because:

- All Sikhs are expected to have a family and technology can be used to bring this about.
- The egg and sperm are from the husband and wife.
- The discarded embryos are not life.
- In AID, egg donation and surrogacy, there are concerns about the identity of the child.

Key points

- Some Sikhs do not allow any of the infertility treatments because they involve taking the life of unwanted embryos.
- Other Sikhs allow IVF and AIH, but are suspicious of all other methods even though they do not ban them.

Evaluation questions

Evaluation questions will only ask you to refer to one religion, so you would be best just to use Christianity in answering evaluation questions, although you could use extra reasons from the other religion you have studied.

Topic 2.9 The nature and importance of transplant surgery

Key points

Transplant surgery is using healthy organs from a donor to replace a dying organ in a patient. It is important because it can give life to dying people and it brings life out of death.

Evaluation questions

You may be required to argue for and against transplant surgery.

1. To argue for, you could use the reasons below right for why transplant surgery is important.

2. To argue against, you could use such reasons as:
   - Surgeons might not try to save the lives of accident victims who they don't know, if they have patients they do know waiting for transplants.
   - Transplant surgery is very expensive and can be used for only a small number of patients.
   - Rich people needing a transplant will be tempted to buy organs from LEDCs.

Main points

Transplant surgery is the use of organs taken from one person and put into another person to replace an organ that is not working. A wide range of organs can now be transplanted successfully (from hearts to eye corneas). Transplant surgery is very effective and gives life and hope to people for whom there is otherwise no hope.

There are two types of transplant surgery – one uses organs from a dead person, the other uses organs from a living person which they can live without (for example, bone-marrow, single kidneys). In the UK, the Unrelated Live Transplant Regulatory Authority (ULTRA) controls live transplants so that people cannot sell their organs.

In June 2008, a government report recommended that the organs of anyone dying in an accident could be used for transplants unless they had a card saying they did not want their organs used (the opposite of the law now). The report estimated that this could double the number of transplant operations.

Why transplant surgery is important

- It cures life-threatening diseases (like kidneys not working) and improves people's lives (like giving sight to blind people).
- Transplants save over 3000 lives a year.
- More people need transplant surgery every year so transplants are essential.
- Transplant surgery gives people a chance to help others after their death by using organs which would otherwise be buried or burned.
- It is pioneering surgical methods which lead to the development of spare part surgery (using artificial organs).

Topic 2.10 Different attitudes to transplant surgery in Christianity

Main points

Most Christians agree with transplant surgery, but would disagree with organs being bought from poor people. This is because:

- Those who believe in immortality of the soul believe the body is not needed after death.
- Those who believe in resurrection believe that God will not need the organs to raise the body.
- Leaving organs for others is a way of loving your neighbour.
- Leaving your organs is a way of treating others as you would want to be treated.
- The Bible says the poor should not be exploited.

Some Christians agree with transplants using organs from living people, but not from dead people. They would also not allow payment for organs. They believe this because:

- Transplanting organs from the dead to the living is playing God which is a great sin.
- Organs such as the heart are an essential part of a person created by God.
- Donating your living organs is a way of loving your neighbour.
- Paying for organs is exploiting the poor which is banned in the Bible.

Some Christians do not agree with transplants at all and do not carry donor cards because:

- They believe it ignores the sanctity of life.
- They believe it is playing God which is a great sin.
- It raises the problem of when someone is dead, and whether the surgeon saves the life of an unknown accident victim or the patient they know who needs a transplant.
- It takes resources from less expensive cures which could help far more people than a single transplant.

Key points

- Some Christians agree with both types of transplant surgery, but not with buying organs from poor people, because they believe the body is not needed after death.
- Some Christians only agree with living transplants because using dead people is 'playing God'.
- Some Christians believe that all forms of transplant surgery are wrong because it is 'playing God'.

Evaluation questions

You may be required to argue for and against Christians/religious people being involved in transplant surgery.

1. To argue for, you could use the first four bullets from most Christians agreeing with transplant surgery above OR the reasons for the importance of transplant surgery in Topic 2.9 (page 34).

2. To argue against, you could use from above the first two bullets from some Christians agreeing with transplants from living donors and the first two bullets from some Christians not agreeing with transplants at all.

Topic 2.11.1 Islam and transplant surgery

As you only need to study one religion, you should only learn one of the four topics on pages 36–37 – the religion you have studied at school.

Key points

- Most Muslims do not agree with transplant surgery because they believe they need all their organs for the Last Day.
- Some Muslims allow transplants from close relatives because it is allowed by some Muslim lawyers.

Main points

Most Muslims do not agree with transplant surgery because:

- The Shari'ah teaches that nothing should be removed from the body after death.
- It is playing God which is the greatest sin of shirk.
- The Qur'an teaches that only God has the right to give and take life.
- It is against Muslim beliefs on the sanctity of life.
- They believe they need all their organs for resurrection on the Last Day.

Some Muslims allow transplants from close relatives because:

- Some Muslim lawyers have said it is allowed.
- The Muslim Law Council of the UK says that Muslims can carry donor cards and have transplants.
- Islam aims to do good and help people.

Topic 2.11.2 Judaism and transplant surgery

Key points

- Most Jewish people agree with transplants from living donors, but not from the dead because organs from non-Jews would alter a person's Jewishness.
- Some Jewish people are against all transplants because they think they are breaking the laws on the sanctity of life.
- Some Jewish people agree with transplants because they save lives and show love of neighbour.

Evaluation questions

Evaluation questions will only ask you to refer to one religion, so you would be best just to use Christianity in answering evaluation questions, although you could use extra reasons from the other religion you have studied.

Main points

Many Jewish people allow transplant surgery using organs from a living Jewish donor because:

- Organs such as the heart are an essential part of the individual God has created.
- Organs from non-Jews would affect a person's Jewishness.
- Giving organs from the dead to the living is playing God which is a great sin.
- Organs from living donors are not as vital and can be used to obey the mitzvah to preserve life.
- Paying for organs is exploiting the poor which is banned by the Tenakh.

Some Jewish people are against all forms of transplant surgery because:

- Transplanting organs is breaking the mitzvot on the sanctity of life.
- Organs have been created by God for a specific person and cannot be swapped around.
- Having non-Jewish organs could change a Jew into a non-Jew.

Some Jewish people agree with transplant surgery, but would not allow payment for organs, because:

- They believe God wants people to use medical technology to save lives.
- They believe that organ donation is a way of obeying the mitzvot to love your neighbour.
- They believe the Tenakh forbids exploiting the poor.

Topic 2.11.3 Hinduism and transplant surgery

Main points

Most Hindus agree with transplant surgery and would carry donor cards because:

- The soul leaves the body on death, so what happens to the organs does not matter.
- The soul is the important part of any individual, so any organs added to the body do not matter.
- Donating your organs to save lives will result in good karma and may lead to moksha.

Some Hindus are against any form of transplant surgery because:

- Transplants break the law of karma; if organs are diseased, that is part of that person's karma.
- Taking an organ from someone else is doing violence to that person which is against the teaching of ahimsa.
- Poor people will be tempted to sell their organs to provide money for the family.

> As you only need to study one religion, you should only learn one of the four topics on pages 36–37 – the religion you have studied at school.

Key points

- Most Hindus allow transplant surgery because they believe that the soul leaves the body at death, so the organs are not needed.
- Some Hindus do not allow transplant surgery because they think it is breaking the law of karma.

Topic 2.11.4 Sikhism and transplant surgery

Main points

Most Sikhs agree with transplants using dead or living donors, but do not agree with organs being paid for because:

- Organ donation is a form of sewa (service) which is very important for Sikhs.
- Guru Nanak said people should leave something to make their good deeds carry on after death.
- They believe the physical body is not needed after death.
- Donating your organs is the best act of charity you can do.

A few Sikhs do not agree with transplant surgery in any form. They have this attitude because:

- It raises the problem of when is someone dead (in heart transplants the heart is removed before it has stopped beating).
- It raises the problem of whether surgeons who have a patient desperate for a transplant will do their best to save the life of a potential donor.
- It tempts poor people to sell their organs to rich people.

Key points

- Most Sikhs agree with both forms of transplant surgery because the body is not needed after death and donation is a form of sewa.
- A few Sikhs do not agree with any transplant surgery because of concerns about when someone is dead and pressures on the living to donate their organs.

Evaluation questions

Evaluation questions will only ask you to refer to one religion, so you would be best just to use Christianity in answering evaluation questions, although you could use extra reasons from the other religion you have studied.

How to answer questions on Section 2

You should already know the basics about how to answer questions from Section 1, pages 16–18, but here is an answer to a whole question on Section 2 with a commentary to help you.

Question a)
What are natural resources? (2 marks)

Answer
Things like oil.

> One mark for a partially correct answer.

Answer
Naturally occurring materials, such as oil and fertile land, which can be used by humans.

> Two marks for a correct definition.

Question b)
Do you think transplant surgery should be allowed? Give TWO reasons for your point of view. (4 marks)

Answer
Yes I do because it cures life-threatening diseases ...

> One mark for a reason.

... like kidneys not working and improves people's lives (like giving sight to the blind).

> Two marks because the reason is developed.

Also, transplant surgery gives people a chance to help others after their death ...

> Three marks because a second reason is given.

... by using organs which would otherwise be buried or burned.

> Four marks because the second reason is developed.

> Total = four marks. Remember! Response questions are really like part (i) of an evaluation question where you only have to give two reasons. To answer a response question, you should just use two reasons from the point of view you agree with in the evaluation questions advice for a topic.

Question c)
Choose one religion other than Christianity and explain why its followers have a duty to look after the Earth. (8 marks)

Answer
Muslims should look after the Earth because their responsibility to be God's khalifah means that Muslims should try to reduce pollution and preserve resources.

> LEVEL 1: two marks for a reason expressed in basic English.

Also, the Shari'ah and ummah tell Muslims that stewardship includes sharing the Earth's resources, so Muslims should work to share the Earth's resources more fairly and improve the standard of living in LEDCs.

> LEVEL 2: by giving a second reason, the answer goes up to level 2 and because the answer is written in clear English it would gain four marks.

The belief that they will be judged on their behaviour as khalifahs means Muslims have a duty to help the work of groups which try to reduce pollution and conserve resources.

> LEVEL 3: by adding another reason the answer moves up to level 3 and because the answer is written in a clear style of English with some use of specialist vocabulary (khalifah, Shari'ah, ummah, sharing resources) it would gain six marks.

Finally, there is a unity and balance in Allah's creation, showing the basic Muslim belief of tawhid. Therefore Muslims have a duty to preserve the environment.

> LEVEL 4: by adding a further reason, the answer moves up to level 4 and because it is written in a clear and correct style of English with extra specialist vocabulary (Allah, creation, tawhid) it would gain eight marks – full marks.

Question d)

'All Christians have the right to have children.'

(i) Do you agree? Give reasons for your opinion. (3 marks)

(ii) Give reasons why some people may disagree with you. (3 marks)

In your answer, you should refer to Christianity.

Answer

(i) I do agree because having children and raising a Christian family is a key purpose of Christian marriage and of the Christian marriage service.

> One mark for a personal opinion with a reason.

Also, it is a part of human nature to want to have children and raise a family, and now infertility treatments can help people achieve this.

> Another reason is given so it moves up to two marks.

Finally, infertility treatments would not be provided by the NHS if having children were not a basic human right.

> The answer now gives another reason for the opinion, so it moves up to three marks.

(ii) Some Christians would disagree with me because they believe that infertility treatments are wrong because many infertility treatments involve fertilising several eggs, some of which are thrown away or used for experimentation. The Catholic Church believes that this is the same as abortion which the Church bans and so they think Christians do not have a right to this.

> One mark for a reason why some people might disagree.

They also think that most forms of infertility treatment involve fertilisation being separated from sex, but God intended procreation to be a part of sex. Therefore they believe Christians do not have a right to have children in this way.

> Another reason is given so it moves up to two marks.

Finally, many Christians believe that infertility may mean that God wants the person to do something other than raise a family, therefore having children is not their right.

> The answer now gives another reason for some people disagreeing, so it moves up to three marks.

> This answer to question d) can gain full marks because part (i) and part (ii) refer to Christianity.

SECTION 2 TEST

SECTION 2: Environmental and medical issues

Answer both questions

1. a) What is organ donation? (2 marks)

   b) Do you think religious people should support organisations like Greenpeace and Friends of the Earth? Give two reasons for your point of view. (4 marks)

   c) Explain why natural resources raise problems for humanity. (8 marks)

   d) 'If everyone were religious, there would be no environmental problems.'
      (i) Do you agree? Give reasons for your opinion. (3 marks)
      (ii) Give reasons why some people may disagree with you. (3 marks)

   In your answer you should refer to at least one religion.

   (Total: 20 marks)

2. a) What is global warming? (2 marks)

   b) Do you think the National Health Service should provide free infertility treatments for couples who cannot have children? Give two reasons for your point of view. (4 marks)

   c) Choose one religion other than Christianity and explain why some of its followers agree with transplant surgery and some do not. (8 marks)

   d) 'Science will solve the problem of resources.'
      (i) Do you agree? Give reasons for your opinion. (3 marks)
      (ii) Give reasons why some people may disagree with you. (3 marks)

   (Total: 20 marks)

You should now use the mark scheme in the Appendix, page 83 to mark your answers, and the self-help tables in the Appendix, pages 84–85 to see how you can improve your performance. If you need more help with the mark scheme for these questions, go to www.hoddereducation.co.uk/religionandsociety

KEY WORDS FOR SECTION 3

Aggression	attacking without being provoked
Bullying	intimidating/frightening people weaker than yourself
Conflict resolution	bringing a fight or struggle to a peaceful conclusion
Exploitation	taking advantage of a weaker group
Forgiveness	stopping blaming someone and/or pardoning them for what they have done wrong
Just war	a war which is fought for the right reasons and in a right way
Pacifism	the belief that all disputes should be settled by peaceful means
Reconciliation	bringing together people who were opposed to each other
Respect	treating a person or their feelings with consideration
The United Nations	an international body set up to promote world peace and cooperation
Weapons of mass destruction	weapons which can destroy large areas and numbers of people
World peace	the ending of war throughout the whole world (the basic aim of the United Nations)

Topic 3.1 The United Nations and world peace

Key points

The United Nations (UN) was formed at the end of the Second World War to preserve world peace. It is important because it brings all the countries of the world together and can send peacekeeping forces to stop conflicts.

The UN sent a peacekeeping force to Kosovo to protect ethnic Albanians from the Serb army and, after keeping the peace for nine years, has helped establish a democratic Kosovar state.

Evaluation questions

You may be required to argue for and against the UN being a good thing.

1. To argue for, you could use any of the ways in which the UN tries to keep world peace and/or its work with the International Criminal Court outlined above right.

2. To argue against, you could look at ways in which the UN has not been able to prevent wars in such places as Iraq, the Democratic Republic of Congo, Darfur, etc.

Main points

The United Nations (UN) was formed at the end of the Second World War to preserve **world peace** and bring about **conflict resolution** by encouraging economic, social, educational and cultural progress throughout the world.

Why the United Nations is important for world peace

Through the Security Council, the UN can try to stop any threats to world peace by:

- imposing sanctions on countries threatening world peace
- authorising the use of force by member states
- sending a UN peacekeeping force to:
  - prevent the outbreak of conflict
  - stabilise conflict situations and bring about a lasting peace agreement
  - help to make peace agreements work
  - bring about stable government (based on democracy and economic development) in conflict areas.

The UN also tries to keep world peace by running the International Criminal Court (ICC) at The Hague which upholds international laws and prosecutes anyone committing war crimes.

One example of the UN's work for peace – Kosovo

One UN field mission was to Kosovo, an area in central Europe with about 80 per cent ethnic Albanians and 20 per cent ethnic Serbs.

Why the UN became involved in Kosovo

When Yugoslavia split up, Kosovo became part of Serbia and the Serbian leader, Slobodan Milosevic, took away Kosovo's self-ruling rights. The Kosovars objected peacefully but failed to get any independence so in the mid-1990s the Kosovans began a guerrilla war. Serbia sent the army into Kosovo and began a campaign of ethnic cleansing against Kosovar Albanians. Hundreds of thousands of refugees fled to Albania, Macedonia and Montenegro. Thousands of people died in the conflict until NATO drove the Serbian forces out in the summer of 1999 and the UN took over the administration of the province.

How the UN dealt with the situation

The UN sent a peacekeeping force to keep the Serbian army out of Kosovo and the Kosovar militias out of the Serb parts of Kosovo. Since 1999 this has protected Kosovar independence and the Serb communities in Kosovo. The UN then worked to set up political parties to allow Kosovar democracy to develop so that in February 2008 the Kosovar leadership seceded from Serbia and Kosovo declared itself an independent democratic state, which has been recognised by most countries other than Serbia and Russia.

Topic 3.2 How religious organisations try to promote world peace

Main points

There are groups in all religions working for world peace such as: Christian Peacemaker teams, Pax Christi International, the Muslim Peace Fellowship, the Jewish Peace Fellowship, Mahatma Gandhi Center for Global Nonviolence and the Sikh Khudai Khidmatgar.

How religious organisations work for world peace

- They organise meetings so that people learn about the horrors of wars and vote for political parties working for peace.
- They organise protests about war (e.g. the Iraq war and the Darfur conflict) to change public opinion and therefore governments' policy.
- They organise and attend inter-faith conferences to help all religions work together to promote world peace.
- They work for economic justice and worldwide acceptance of human rights to remove the causes of war. If the poor of the world had a decent standard of living, and the governments of the world respected human rights, this could stop many wars.

Key points

There are organisations working for world peace in all the world's religions. They try to promote world peace by:

- going to war zones and supporting efforts to stop the war
- organising demonstrations against wars
- educating people about the need for world peace.

Evaluation questions

You may be required to argue for and against religious organisations doing more for world peace than anyone else.

1. To argue for, you could use any of the above bullets about how religious organisations work for world peace.

2. To argue against, you could look at the work of the UN for world peace in Topic 3.1 (page 42) and argue that it is more effective than the religious organisations.

Topic 3.3 Why wars occur

Key points

Wars can occur for a number of reasons including:

- religion (for example, if followers of a religion are being badly treated in another country)
- nationalism and ethnicity (for example, if an ethnic group wants to set up its own country)
- economics (for example, if a country has oil but its neighbour does not)
- political reasons (for example, if one country is communist and wants to make other countries communist).

Evaluation questions

You may be required to argue for and against it being possible to end wars.

1. To argue for, you could use such argument as:
   - If religions came together in a search for peace and unity, religious wars would stop.
   - If we had a world federation of states (a world version of the EU or the USA), wars caused by nationalism and political differences would disappear.
   - If we had a fair sharing of the Earth's resources, economic wars would end.

2. To argue against, you could use any of the bullets from the main points on the right and explain why wars will never disappear.

Main points

1 Religion

Wars often occur because of religious differences.

- If the followers of a religion are being badly treated in a country, the followers in another country might invade to protect them. For example, Serbia invaded Kosovo to protect the Orthodox Christians from the Muslim majority.
- Most of a country is one religion, but an area of the country is a different religion. For example, the Muslims of Kashmir are fighting to leave India to become part of Muslim Pakistan.
- There are differences within a religion and one religious group attacks the other for having different beliefs, for example the Taliban view of Islam attacking other views of Islam in Afghanistan.

2 Nationalism and ethnicity

A major cause of wars is connected with nationalism and ethnicity:

- The belief that each separate ethnic group should have its own country leads to wars such as the Tamil Tigers in Sri Lanka and the ethnic Albanians in Kosovo.
- This can also lead to the belief that any minority ethnic groups should be removed from the country as happened in Rwanda in 1994.
- Where countries were created artificially, tensions between ethnic groups can lead to civil wars. Sudan and Kenya were created artificially by European conquerors, leading to the current war in Darfur.

3 Economics

Wars can often occur because of arguments about resources:

- Some people think that Iraq was invaded because the West wanted access to its oil reserves.
- The economic crisis in Zimbabwe has led to mass migration of refugees into South Africa. Some South Africans have begun to attack the refugees to protect their jobs.

4 Ideological and political differences

Wars can sometimes occur because of differences about ideals or politics:

- In the Democratic Republic of the Congo two different political groups are fighting each other for power. The UN is trying to bring peace but (at the time of writing) the conflict has become very serious.
- The Korean war began in 1949 when communist North Korea invaded capitalist South Korea. The UN sent a force to protect the South, and a truce was declared in 1953 but there is still no peace.

Topic 3.4 The nature and importance of the theory of just war

Main points

Although most people agree that wars are bad because of their effects, most people also agree that some wars can be justified. The theory used to decide whether a war is justified is known as the **just war** theory.

Today it is generally agreed that a war is just if:
- The cause of the war is just (for example, it is fought in self-defence when another country attacks).
- It is being fought by the authority of the UN.
- It is being fought with the intention to bring back peace.
- It is begun as a last resort – all other ways of ending the conflict have been tried and failed.
- There is a reasonable chance of success.
- The methods used avoid killing civilians.
- The methods used are proportional to the cause. For example, it would not be just to destroy a country with **weapons of mass destruction** because it had invaded a small island.

Key points

The just war theory is the idea that it is right to go to war if the reasons are just. For example, it has been agreed to by the UN, or it is being fought in self-defence.

Evaluation questions

Any evaluation questions on the just war will require you to refer to religion, and so they are dealt with after the next topic.

Topic 3.5 Differences among Christians in their attitudes to war

Key points

- Some Christians believe that they should work for peace by refusing to fight in wars. They believe Christians should be pacifists because Jesus taught Christians to love their enemies.
- Some Christians believe that the way to bring peace is to be prepared to fight in just wars. They will fight to defend the weak and to bring peace to the world because this has always been the Church's teaching.

Evaluation questions

You may be required to argue for and against religious people being able to fight in just wars.

1. To argue for, you should use the reasons why Christians can fight in just wars, given on the right.

2. To argue against, you should use the reasons for Christian pacifism given above right.

Main points

There are two very different Christian attitudes to war.

1 Christian pacifism

Pacifism means refusing to fight in wars. There are many Christian pacifist groups, the largest being the Catholic group Pax Christi. The Quakers, Plymouth Brethren and Christadelphians are completely pacifist Churches. These Christians are pacifists because:

- Jesus said Christians should love their enemies and turn the other cheek when attacked.
- The fifth commandment says 'Do not kill'.
- Jesus would not let Peter fight back when Jesus was being arrested.
- Horrible things happen to innocent civilians in modern wars.
- They believe that peace can only come when people refuse to fight.
- Modern warfare affects so many innocent people, so modern wars can never be justified.

2 The attitude that Christians can fight in just wars

All Christians believe that they are called to bring peace to the world, but many Christians believe that the way to work for peace is to be prepared to fight a just war (see Topic 3.4, page 45). They believe they can fight in just wars because:

- It is the teaching of most of the Churches (Catholic, Anglican, Methodist, Baptist, URC).
- St Paul said that Christians have to obey the orders of the government, so Christians should fight in wars ordered by the government.
- Jesus did not condemn soldiers, he actually praised the faith of a Roman centurion.
- They believe that if we need a police force to protect innocent people against criminals, we need armed forces to protect innocent states against criminal ones.

Topic 3.6.1 Islam and attitudes to war

Main points

There is no idea of pacifism in Islam. The Qur'an encourages all Muslims to 'struggle in the way of Islam' (jihad). Muslims believe in two forms of jihad: the greater jihad is the struggle to make yourself and your society perfectly Muslim; the lesser jihad is fighting in a just war.

Most Muslims believe that if a war is just then a Muslim should fight in it because:

- The Qur'an says that Muslims must fight if they are attacked.
- Muhammad fought in wars.
- There are many hadith from Muhammad saying Muslims should fight in just wars.
- The Qur'an says that a Muslim who dies in a just war will go straight to heaven.

However, some Muslims feel that the nature of modern weapons means that no war can be a just war, and so they oppose wars.

As you only need to study one religion, you should only learn one of the four topics on pages 47–49 – the religion you have studied at school.

Key points

Muslims believe in peace, but Islam teaches that if the faith is attacked, Muslims must defend their faith by fighting jihad (a just war fought in a just way). They believe this because it is taught in the Qur'an, which they believe is the word of God.

Topic 3.6.2 Judaism and attitudes to war

Main points

Peace is the ideal for all Jews. However, Judaism expects Jews to fight in just wars because:

- The Talmud says war must be fought if God commands it.
- There are mitzvot saying that Jews must fight when attacked.
- There are many accounts in the Tenakh of how Israel had to fight wars to preserve its independence.
- The Holocaust reminds Jews what can happen if there is no army to defend Jews against attack.

However, there are some Jewish pacifists who believe that war is wrong in the modern world because modern weapons are bound to harm so many innocent people.

Key points

Jews believe in peace, but Judaism teaches that Jews must defend themselves if they are attacked, as stated in the Torah and Talmud. However, some Jews are pacifists because they think modern weapons are too destructive ever to be used.

Evaluation questions

Evaluation questions will only ask you to refer to one religion, so you would be best just to use Christianity in answering evaluation questions, although you could use extra reasons from the other religion you have studied.

47

Topic 3.6.3 Hinduism and attitudes to war

As you only need to study one religion, you should only learn one of the four topics on pages 47–49 – the religion you have studied at school.

Key points

All Hindus believe in peace, but there are different attitudes to war in Hinduism:

- Some Hindus will not take part in any wars because they believe they should follow ahimsa (non-violence).
- Some Hindus think it is right to fight if attacked because this is taught in scriptures such as the Bhagavad Gita.

Evaluation questions

Evaluation questions will only ask you to refer to one religion, so you would be best just to use Christianity in answering evaluation questions, although you could use extra reasons from Hinduism.

Main points

Although Hinduism is dedicated to peace, there are two different attitudes to war among Hindus.

1 Pacifism and non-violence

Some Hindus believe that violence in any form is wrong because:

- The Hindu belief of ahimsa means non-violence.
- Killing people puts a person's soul further from moksha.
- Gandhi's struggle for Indian independence from the British showed pacifism can work as a way of removing injustice.
- Modern methods of warfare are so terrible that they are bound to take innocent lives, which is against all the teachings of Hinduism.

2 The Hindu just war

Many Hindus believe that it is right to fight in wars to resist attack or to remove great injustice. They believe this because:

- The second Hindu caste is the warrior caste whose duty (karma) is to defend Hinduism.
- The Gita says that Hindus must fight in just wars as killing people does not kill their souls.
- There are many stories in the Hindu Scriptures of Hindu gods being involved in wars when they came to Earth.
- The Laws of Manu set out strict rules about just wars, so they must be allowed for Hindus.

So Hindus have a similar problem to Christians. Most probably accept the need to fight just wars, but many Hindus are opposed to war in any form.

Topic 3.6.4 Sikhism and attitudes to war

Main points

Sikhs are strongly in favour of action to promote human rights and harmony between religions and states, but most Sikhs agree with fighting in just wars because:

- From the time of the fifth Guru, the Gurus used armies to stop oppression and attempts to destroy the Sikh faith.
- The sixth guru, Guru Har Gobind, said that armies could be used to promote the cause of justice and protect the innocent.
- The tenth Guru, Guru Gobind Singh, formed the khalsa whose members carry a Kirpan (sword) to 'righteously defend the fine line of the Truth'.
- Guru Gobind Singh said military action should be a last resort, but should not be avoided if necessary.
- The Rahit Maryada teaches that Sikhs should fight in wars which fulfil the requirements of the 'Dharam Yudh' (war in the defence of righteousness).

However, some Sikhs (such as the Khudai Khidmatgar) believe that Guru Nanak was against war and that no war can be a just war using modern weapons, and so they oppose wars.

As you only need to study one religion, you should only learn one of the four topics on pages 47–49 – the religion you have studied at school.

Key points

Sikhs are not pacifists and are expected to fight to protect the oppressed and human rights. However, the war must be fought justly. Just wars must be fought by Sikhs even if there is no chance of success.

Evaluation questions

Evaluation questions will only ask you to refer to one religion, so you would be best just to use Christianity in answering evaluation questions, although you could use extra reasons from Sikhism.

Topic 3.7 Christian attitudes to bullying

Key points

Bullying is when stronger people pick on weak people to make their lives miserable. Bullying can lead to stress, nervous breakdown, even suicide.

Christians are against bullying because it is the duty of Christians to protect the innocent and it is sinful for Christians to use violence without a just cause.

Main points

What is bullying?

Bullying is frightening people who are weaker than you. Most people connect bullying with school and school bullying can include: name calling, pinching, kicking, hitting, taking possessions, ignoring people or leaving them out of games, sending abusive texts or e-mails, abusing people because of their religion, ethnic origin, appearance, sexuality or disability.

Why Christians are against bullying

- Christianity regards using **aggression** or violence without a just cause as sinful.
- Christians believe people are a creation of God made in God's image. Bullying is mistreating God's creation and so is wrong.
- It is the duty of Christians to protect the weak and innocent (for example, the Parable of the Good Samaritan), but bullies do the exact opposite and so must be wrong.
- Jesus taught that Christians should treat anyone in trouble as if they were Jesus. No Christian would bully Jesus and so they should not bully anyone.
- All the Christian Churches teach that Christians should protect human rights and so they should not bully because bullying denies the victim's human rights.
- Bullying has harmful effects on society, and Christians should always try to make society better.

Evaluation questions

You may be required to argue for and against Christians having a duty to stand up to bullies.

1. To argue for, you should use any of the reasons above for why Christians are against bullying.

2. Christians who disagree are likely to use such reasons as:

- It is more important for Christians to help the victims of bullying (loving their neighbour).
- Unless they are very strong, standing up to bullies could make the bullies even worse as they might bully the person standing up to them.
- It is always better to use the forces of law and order to stand up to criminals (which is what bullies are).

Topic 3.8.1 Islam and attitudes to bullying

Main points

Muslims are against all forms of bullying because:

- Islamic society is based on **respect** between the members of society. Bullies have no respect for the people they bully and so do not understand Islamic society.
- Islam regards using violence without a just cause as sinful.
- Any Muslim who bullies a fellow Muslim is acting against the ummah.
- It is the duty of Muslims to protect the weak and innocent but bullies do the exact opposite and so must be wrong.
- Muhammad said, 'Every Muslim is a brother to every Muslim.' No one should bully their brother and so Muslims should not bully anyone.
- All the law schools teach that Muslims should defend human rights and bullying denies the victim's human rights.

As you only need to study one religion, you should only learn one of the four topics on pages 51–52 – the religion you have studied at school.

Key points

Muslims are against bullying because Muslims should be responsible citizens. They should treat all Muslims as their brothers and they should protect the weak and innocent.

Topic 3.8.2 Judaism and attitudes to bullying

Main points

Jewish people are against all forms of bullying because:

- Jewish society is based on respect between the members of society. Bullies have no respect for the people they bully and so do not understand Jewish society.
- Judaism regards using violence without a just cause as sinful.
- Judaism teaches that people are a creation of God made in God's image. Bullying is mistreating God's creation and so is wrong.
- It is the duty of Jewish people to protect the weak and innocent but bullies do the exact opposite and so must be wrong.
- All the different forms of Judaism teach that Jewish people should defend human rights and bullying denies the victim's human rights.

Key points

Jewish people are against bullying because they should love their neighbours and protect the weak and innocent who were created by God in his image.

Evaluation questions

Evaluation questions will only ask you to refer to one religion, so you would be best just to use Christianity in answering evaluation questions, although you could use extra reasons from the other religion you have studied.

Topic 3.8.3 Hinduism and attitudes to bullying

As you only need to study one religion, you should only learn one of the four topics on pages 51–52 – the religion you have studied at school.

Key points

Hindus are against bullying because it involves violence which is against belief in ahimsa. It also brings bad karma which will delay moksha. It is also denying the victim's human rights which Hindus should protect.

Main points

Hindus are against all forms of bullying because:

- Hindu society is based on respect between the members of society. Bullies have no respect for the people they bully and so do not understand Hindu society.
- Bullying is against the doctrine of ahimsa (non-violence) and so is sinful.
- Bullying is mistreating the divine essence which is inside everyone. It will bring bad karma, which will prevent the bully from gaining moksha.
- It is the duty of Hindus to protect the weak as this brings good karma, making it easier to gain moksha. Bullying is the exact opposite of this and so must be wrong.
- All Hindus believe they should defend human rights but bullying denies the victim's human rights.

Topic 3.8.4 Sikhism and attitudes to bullying

Key points

Sikhs are against bullying because it involves unlawful violence, which is manmukh rather than gurmukh. It also brings bad karma, which will delay mukti. It is also denying the victim's human rights, which Sikhs should protect.

Evaluation questions

Evaluation questions will only ask you to refer to one religion, so you would be best just to use Christianity in answering evaluation questions, although you could use extra reasons from the other religion you have studied.

Main points

Sikhs are against all forms of bullying because:

- Sikh society is based on respect between the members of society. Bullies have no respect for the people they bully and so do not understand Sikh society.
- Bullying is manmukh (human centred) rather than gurmukh (living by the Gurus' teachings).
- Bullying uses unjustified violence which is sinful.
- Bullying is mistreating the divine essence which is inside everyone. It will bring bad karma, which will prevent the bully from gaining mukti.
- It is the duty of Sikhs to protect the weak as this brings good karma, making it easier to gain mukti. Bullying is the exact opposite of this and so must be wrong.
- All Sikhs believe they should defend human rights but bullying denies the victim's human rights.

Topic 3.9 Religious conflicts within families

Main points

The main ways in which religion can cause conflicts within families are as follows.

1 Children no longer wanting to take part in their parents' religion

If parents are religious, but the children are not, it causes conflict because:

- Religions tell parents to bring their children up in the faith and make sure they become full members of it as adults.
- Parents worry that without religion their children will become immoral.
- Parents worry that they will not see children in the after-life.

2 Children wanting to marry a partner from a different faith

In a multi-faith society, young people of different faiths fall in love and want to marry which causes conflict because:

- Often there can be no religious wedding ceremony if they are not the same religion.
- There is a question of which religion the children of the marriage will be brought up in.
- Parents feel their children have betrayed them by falling in love with someone from a different religion.

3 Children becoming more religious than their parents

Often parents do not follow their religion very strictly. If their children decide to be strict followers, this can cause conflict. For example:

- if the child wants to have a low-paid job as a priest (minister), imam, charity worker, or joins a religious community and is not allowed to marry
- if the child criticises the parents (Catholic parents using contraception, Muslim parents running off-licences, Hindu parents eating beef)
- if the child tries to force the parents to be more religious, for example Baptist children saying parents should read the Bible every day, Sikh children stopping their parents from drinking alcohol.

4 Disagreements over moral issues

Moral decisions can cause major arguments. For example:

- if a Catholic or a Sikh decides to divorce and marry someone else
- if a couple decide to live together rather than marrying
- if a family member decides to have an abortion.

Key points

Conflicts can occur in families if children:

- no longer wish to follow their parents' religion, but the parents want them to
- want to marry someone of a different religion
- become more religious than their parents and start criticising their parents for not following the religion strictly enough
- disagree with their parents over moral issues.

Evaluation questions

You may be required to argue for and against religion causing conflict within families.

1. To argue for, you could use any of the points on the left.

2. To argue against, you could use such reasons as:
   - Religion brings families together as they worship together and have a social life together.
   - Children brought up in a religion are likely to believe it and so it won't bring conflict.
   - Most religious parents respect their children's right to freedom of religion when they are old enough so it does not cause conflict.

Topic 3.10 Christian teachings on forgiveness and reconciliation

Key points

Christians believe they should forgive those who attack them or hurt them. They also believe they should try to settle conflicts and bring reconciliation between people. They believe this because Jesus taught forgiveness and reconciliation.

Main points

Christians believe in **forgiveness** and **reconciliation** because:

- Jesus died on the cross to bring reconciliation and forgiveness.
- Jesus said that if Christians do not forgive others, they will not be forgiven themselves.
- St Paul said that Christians should try to live in peace with everyone.
- All the Churches teach that Christians should use forgiveness and reconciliation to end conflicts.

However, Christians believe that a conflict about a moral or religious issue would not be able to be resolved, for example, if parents argued that a Roman Catholic son should not become a priest.

Evaluation questions

You may be required to argue for and against Christians having a duty to forgive enemies/bullies/those who wrong them.

1. To argue for, you could use any of the reasons above for Christians believing in forgiveness and reconciliation.

2. Christians who disagree are likely to use such reasons as:

- Christians cannot be expected to forgive those who hate them.
- Christians should fight against evil and so they should oppose not forgive enemies/bullies/those who wrong them.
- Christians are human and it is not natural for humans to forgive enemies/bullies/those who wrong them.

Topic 3.11.1 Islam: teachings on forgiveness and reconciliation

Main points

Muslims believe they should be forgiving and try to bring reconciliation because:

- God is compassionate and merciful to sinners, so Muslims should also be forgiving.
- How can Muslims ask for God's forgiveness on the Last Day if they are not prepared to forgive people?
- The Qur'an says that Muslims should forgive those who offend them.
- Muhammad said in many hadith that Muslims should be forgiving.

However, Muslims should not forgive those who work against Islam.

As you only need to study one religion, you should only learn one of the four topics on pages 55–56 – the religion you have studied at school.

Key points

Muslims try to forgive those who wrong them and try to resolve conflicts because this is the teaching of the Qur'an. Muslims are also taught to forgive if they expect God to forgive them.

Topic 3.11.2 Judaism: teachings on forgiveness and reconciliation

Main points

Jews believe they should be forgiving and try to bring reconciliation because:

- The Tenakh teaches that God forgives those who turn to him in repentance.
- The Tenakh teaches that Jews should forgive those who wrong them.
- Rabbis encourage Jews to forgive those who wrong them.
- It is Jewish belief that Jews should forgive those who have wronged them, when on their deathbed, so that God will forgive their sins.
- In the days between Rosh Hashanah and Yom Kippur Jews have to settle any quarrels they have had with families or friends over the past year.

However, Jewish people do not have to forgive the enemies of Judaism, nor people who don't want to be forgiven.

Key points

Jews believe they should forgive those who wrong them because it is taught in the Tenakh. They also believe it is their duty to resolve conflicts as every year they have Yom Kippur when they must forgive people and resolve any personal conflicts.

Evaluation questions

Evaluation questions will only ask you to refer to one religion, so you would be best just to use Christianity in answering evaluation questions, although you could use extra reasons from the other religion you have studied.

Topic 3.11.3 Hinduism: teachings on forgiveness and reconciliation

As you only need to study one religion, you should only learn one of the four topics on pages 55–56 – the religion you have studied at school.

Key points

All Hindus believe they should try to bring reconciliation to conflicts to gain good karma. However, some Hindus think the law of cause and effect (karma) means no forgiveness; others believe that forgiving others is the way to moksha.

Main points

Some Hindus do not believe in forgiveness and reconciliation because everything is a result of karma and people's karma cannot be changed.

Most Hindus believe in forgiveness and reconciliation because:

- In the gunas, forgiveness is a quality of light which leads the soul to moksha.
- The Upanishads teach that it is dangerous for the soul not to forgive.
- Many swamis believe that forgiveness is a part of moksha.
- It is better for one's soul to forgive as unforgiving souls go backwards in samsara.

Topic 3.11.4 Sikhism: teachings on forgiveness and reconciliation

Key points

Sikhism believes in forgiveness and reconciliation wherever possible because this was the teaching and example of the Gurus. The Adi Granth encourages Sikhs to be merciful and forgiving; and the Paryushana Parva Mela is all about forgiving those who have wronged you.

Evaluation questions

Evaluation questions will only ask you to refer to one religion, so you would be best just to use Christianity in answering evaluation questions, although you could use extra reasons from the other religion you have studied.

Main points

Sikhs believe in forgiveness and reconciliation because:

- Sikhism began because Guru Nanak wanted to reconcile the religions of Islam and Hinduism that divided India.
- There are many examples of the Gurus showing forgiveness and seeking reconciliation.
- The Adi Granth teaches the importance of forgiveness and reconciliation.
- The festival of Paryushana Parva celebrates friendship and forgiveness.
- The holy books teach that forgiveness and reconciliation cannot be separated.

However, Sikhs believe that a conflict over moral or religious issues might not be able to be resolved, for example if Sikhs were criticising the khalsa.

How to answer questions on Section 3

You should already know the basics about how to answer questions from Section 1, pages 16–18, but here is an answer to a whole question on Section 3 with a commentary to help you.

Question a)
What is exploitation? (2 marks)

Answer
Ripping people off.

> One mark for a partially correct answer.

Answer
Taking advantage of a weaker group.

> Two marks for a correct definition.

Question b)
Do you think war can ever be justified?
Give TWO reasons for your point of view. (4 marks)

Answer
Yes because I am a Muslim and the Qur'an says that Muslims must fight if they are attacked ...

> One mark for a reason.

... and the Qur'an is the word of God which Muslims should follow.

> Two marks because the reason is developed.

Also, Muhammad fought in wars ...

> Three marks because a second reason is given.

... and it is the duty of Muslims to follow the example of Muhammad the perfect exemplar.

> Four marks because the second reason is developed.

> Total = four marks. Remember! Response questions are really like part (i) of an evaluation question where you only have to give two reasons. To answer a response question, you should just use two reasons from the point of view you agree with in the evaluation questions advice for a topic.

Question c)
Choose one religion other than Christianity and explain why its followers should forgive people. (8 marks)

Answer
Hindus should forgive those who wrong them because in the gunas, forgiveness is a quality of light which leads the soul to moksha.

> LEVEL 1: two marks for a reason expressed in basic English.

Also, the Upanishads teach that it is dangerous for the soul not to forgive and the Upanishads are Smriti scriptures and so should be obeyed.

> LEVEL 2: by giving a second reason, the answer goes up to level 2 and because the answer is written in clear English it would gain four marks.

Furthermore, many swamis have taught that forgiveness is a part of moksha, the goal of all Hindus.

> LEVEL 3: by adding another reason the answer moves up to level 3 and because the answer is written in a clear style of English with some use of specialist vocabulary (gunas, moksha, Upanishads, Smriti, swami) it would gain six marks.

Finally, most Hindus believe that it is better for one's soul to forgive as unforgiving souls go backwards in samsara. This means that if they do not forgive, they will be reincarnated and not reach moksha.

> LEVEL 4: by adding a further reason, the answer moves up to level 4 and because it is written in a clear and correct style of English with extra specialist vocabulary (soul, unforgiving, samsara, reincarnated) it would gain eight marks – full marks.

Question d)

'Religion causes more conflict in families than anything else.'

(i) Do you agree? Give reasons for your opinion.   (3 marks)
(ii) Give reasons why some people may disagree with you.   (3 marks)

In your answer, you should refer to at least one religion.

Answer

One mark for a personal opinion with a reason.

(i) I do agree because I have Christian friends and I can see the conflicts it causes in their families. For example, if children don't want to go to church, it causes conflict because at baptism the parents promised to bring their children up in the faith and make sure they become full members of it as adults.

Another reason is given so it moves up to two marks.

Also, if they wanted to marry someone from a different religion, it would cause problems because there could be no religious wedding ceremony and the parents would want them to marry in church.

The answer now gives another reason for the opinion, so it moves up to three marks.

Finally, moral decisions can cause major arguments. For example, some people I know decided to live together rather than marrying, and their Christian parents would not speak to them because they thought they were living in sin.

One mark for a reason. Why some people might disagree.

(ii) Christians would disagree with me because they believe that other issues cause more conflict in families than religion. For example, wanting to marry someone of a different skin colour would cause major problems in some families.

Another reason is given so it moves up to two marks.

Politics can cause major family problems. Imagine what a right-wing politician would feel if their child became a communist.

The answer now gives another reason for some people disagreeing, so it moves up to three marks.

Finally, they may argue that moral issues can cause just as much conflict in a non-religious family as in a religious one. Someone wanting an abortion, or wanting to live with someone could cause great conflict in a non-religious family with traditional values.

This answer to question d) can gain full marks because part (i) refers to Christianity.

SECTION 3 TEST

SECTION 3: Peace and conflict

Answer both questions

1. a) What is aggression? (2 marks)

   b) Do you think religion is the best way to bring about world peace? Give two reasons for your point of view. (4 marks)

   c) Choose one religion other than Christianity and explain why some of its followers believe they should fight in just wars. (8 marks)

   d) 'Religious people should always forgive those who wrong them.'
   (i) Do you agree? Give reasons for your opinion. (3 marks)
   (ii) Give reasons why some people may disagree with you. (3 marks)

   In your answer you should refer to at least one religion.

   (Total: 20 marks)

2. a) What is the United Nations? (2 marks)

   b) Do you think religious people should fight in wars? Give two reasons for your point of view. (4 marks)

   c) Choose one religion other than Christianity and explain why it is opposed to bullying. (8 marks)

   d) 'No Christian should ever fight in wars.'
   (i) Do you agree? Give reasons for your opinion. (3 marks)
   (ii) Give reasons why some people may disagree with you. (3 marks)

   In your answer you should refer to Christianity.

   (Total: 20 marks)

You should now use the mark scheme in the Appendix, page 83 to mark your answers, and the self-help tables in the Appendix, pages 84–85 to see how you can improve your performance. If you need more help with the mark scheme for these questions, go to www.hoddereducation.co.uk/religionandsociety

Section 4 **Crime and punishment**

KEY WORDS FOR SECTION 4

Addiction	a recurring compulsion to engage in an activity regardless of its bad effects
Capital punishment	the death penalty for a crime or offence
Crime	an act against the law
Deterrence	the idea that punishments should be of such a nature that they will put people off (deter) committing crimes
Judgement	the act of judging people and their actions
Justice	due allocation of reward and punishment/ the maintenance of what is right
Law	rules made by Parliament and enforceable by the courts
Reform	the idea that punishments should try to change criminals so that they will not commit crimes again
Rehabilitation	restore to normal life
Responsibility	being responsible for one's actions
Retribution	the idea that punishments should make criminals pay for what they have done wrong
Sin	an act against the will of God

Topic 4.1 The need for law and justice

Main points

Laws are rules about how people are expected to behave. The courts and the police make sure that all members of society obey the law.

Why do we need laws?

- We need laws so that people know what sort of behaviour to expect from each other. If there were no rules there would be chaos. For example, on the roads, people could drive on the right or the left, at any speed they liked, through red lights, etc.
- If there were no laws about business deals and work, modern-day society could not operate. Would you bother to work if you weren't sure you would be paid? Would you make things if people took them without paying you?
- We need laws to protect the weak from the strong. Imagine what life would be like if there were no laws on stealing, murder and rape. The British philosopher Thomas Hobbes said that without laws, life would be 'nasty, brutish and short'.
- In an advanced civilisation such as the UK's, we need laws to keep everything organised.

Why does there need to be a connection between the law and justice?

- If a law is unjust, people will feel that it is right to break the law.
- If some laws are unjust, then they are not fulfilling their purpose of making sure that people are rewarded for their work, the weak are protected, etc.
- If a law is unjust, people will not obey it and will campaign against the law, causing trouble in society.
- If the laws do not create a just society, people will think the legal system is not working and may start a civil war (for example, Kosovo where the Kosovars began a civil war because they thought the Serbian legal system was treating them unfairly).
- This means that, if laws are unjust, they will disrupt rather than unite society.

Key points

Society needs laws for it to work properly and to protect the weak from the strong. The laws need to be just so that people will obey them and feel that they make society better.

Evaluation questions

You may be required to argue for and against society needing laws.

1. To argue that we do need laws, you could use any of the reasons on the left for why do we need laws.

2. To argue against, you could use such reasons as:
   - Laws restrict human freedom and individuals should be free to do as they wish.
   - Some countries have experimented with getting rid of traffic laws in towns and have found there are fewer accidents.
   - Small societies work well without laws because people know each other and know how to treat each other without having any laws.

Evaluation questions

You may be required to argue for and against there needing to be a connection between laws and justice.

1. To argue for, you could use any of the reasons from why there needs to be a connection between laws and justice above.

2. To argue against, you could use such reasons as:
   - The main thing is for everyone to know what the laws are. As long as people know what the law is they can obey it whether it is just or not.
   - Laws are there to help society to function; whether they are just or not does not matter as long as the laws work.
   - Often there is no agreement on what is just and some people may think a law is just while others think it is unjust.

Topic 4.2 Theories of punishment

Key points

The main theories of punishment are:

- retribution – that criminals should be punished for what they have done
- deterrence – that punishments should be so harsh no one would dare commit a crime
- reformation – that punishment should try to change criminals into law-abiding citizens
- protection – that punishments should protect society from criminals.

Main points

If law is to work, there must be punishments for those who break the laws. In the UK, when someone is found guilty of a **crime**, a judge or magistrate makes a **judgement** on what their punishment should be. There are different theories about what punishment should do.

Retribution is the theory that criminals should pay for their crime because:

- It makes criminals pay for their crime in proportion to the severity of the crime committed. In the past retributive punishments would have killed those who committed murder and taken the eyes out of those who blinded someone.
- It makes criminals suffer for what they have done wrong.
- It actually punishes the criminal.

Deterrence is the theory that the punishment should put people off committing crime. The idea of deterrent punishment is that punishment should be so severe no one will dare to commit crimes. For example:

- If people know thieves have their hand cut off, then they will not steal.
- If people know murderers will be executed, they will not murder.

Reform is the theory that criminals should be taught not to commit crime again. Many people think this is the best punishment because:

- The only way to stop crime is to turn criminals into honest law-abiding citizens.
- Most criminals have had a bad upbringing and they do not know how to live without crime.
- Reformative punishments give criminals education and qualifications so that they can find a proper job (**rehabilitation of offenders**).

Protection is the theory that punishment should protect society from criminals. For example:

- **Capital punishment** is a good punishment for murderers because if they are dead they cannot kill anyone else.
- Long prison sentences keep criminals out of society so that people and property are protected.
- Community service keeps hooligans and vandals off the streets in their leisure time.

Most forms of punishment are a mixture of theories. Prison can deter, protect, inflict retribution and give reformation.

Evaluation questions

You may be required to argue for and against retribution/deterrence/reform as being the best form of punishment.

1. To argue for, you could use the reasons given on page 62 for the relevant theory.

2. To argue against retribution, you could use such reasons as:
   - Applying retribution is making you as bad as the criminal because you are doing the same thing.
   - Retribution will not stop criminals from re-offending.
   - Retribution was condemned by Jesus in the Sermon on the Mount.

   To argue against deterrence, you could use such reasons as:

   - People who are going to commit a crime do not think they will get caught and so will not be deterred by the punishment.
   - Evidence from countries with the death penalty shows they have higher murder rates than countries which do not, so it does not seem to deter.
   - Countries which cut off the hands of thieves do not have less theft because poor people steal to keep their families alive.

   To argue against reform, you could use such reasons as:

   - Reform does not work with many criminals as they re-offend.
   - Psychopaths, etc. cannot be reformed.
   - Reform methods can be much more expensive than other forms of punishment.

Topic 4.3 Why justice is important for Christians

Key points

Christians believe justice is important because the Bible says God is a God of justice who will reward the good and punish the bad at the end of the world. The Bible and the Churches encourage Christians to work for justice by campaigning for fair treatment for the poor, etc.

Main points

Justice has always been an important issue in Christianity because:

- The Bible says that God is just and will reward the righteous (another word for those who are just) and punish those who sin.
- The Bible says that people should be treated fairly, and that God wants the world to be ruled justly.
- There are many statements in the New Testament about how Christians should treat people fairly and equally.
- The Christian Churches have made many statements about the need for Christians to work for justice.
- The Christian Churches organised the successful Jubilee 2000 campaign to persuade the governments of the rich countries to cancel the debts of poor countries as they believed it was unjust. The Christian campaign for justice goes on under the name Jubilee Research.
- The World Council of Churches says Churches across the world should work for 'Justice, peace and the integrity of creation'.

Evaluation questions

You may be required to argue for and against justice being more important for religious people.

1. To argue for, you could use any of the reasons why justice is important for Christians, given above.

2. To argue that it is important for everyone, not just religious people, you could use any of the points from why there needs to be a connection between laws and justice in Topic 4.1 (page 61).

Topic 4.4.1 Why justice is important for Muslims

Main points

Justice is important for Muslims because:

- The Qur'an says God is just.
- The Qur'an says that Muslims should treat people fairly.
- Muslims believe it is part of their role as vice-gerents of God's creation to treat all people fairly.
- The Shari'ah is based on justice for everyone with everyone being treated equally.
- Islam teaches that it is unjust to be involved in the charging of interest because it takes money from the poor and gives it to the rich.

As you only need to study one religion, you should only learn one of the four topics on pages 65–66 – the religion you have studied at school.

Key points

Muslims believe in justice because the Qur'an says that God is just, and the Shari'ah says Muslims must work for justice through zakah if they are to go to heaven on the Last Day.

Topic 4.4.2 Why justice is important for Jews

Main points

Justice is important for Jewish people because:

- God is just, and God created the world as a place of justice.
- Jews have to live their lives according to the mitzvot (laws) and so it is important for the courts to operate fairly and for everyone to be treated equally.
- The Torah says that God is a God of justice and for Jewish people the Torah is the word of God.
- The Tenakh says that people should be treated fairly and not cheated and there are many statements in the Responsa about how Jews should treat people fairly and equally.
- As part of their belief in justice, Jews have been very involved in the struggle for equal rights and the change of unjust laws (many American Jews worked for the civil rights movement for equal rights for black Americans and many Russian Jews campaigned for human rights in the former USSR).

Key points

Jews believe in justice because the Torah says God is a God of justice and the Tenakh encourages Jewish people to work for justice by working for fair shares for the poor.

Evaluation questions

Evaluation questions will only ask you to refer to one religion, so you would be best just to use Christianity in answering evaluation questions, although you could use extra reasons from the other religion you have studied.

Topic 4.4.3 Why justice is important for Hindus

As you only need to study one religion, you should only learn one of the four topics on pages 65–66 – the religion you have studied at school.

Key points

Justice is important for Hindus because it is the basis of beliefs in dharma and samsara. Many Hindus believe they should work for justice because this cleans their soul so they can gain moksha.

Main points

Justice is important for Hindus because:

- In order to gain moksha, Hindus must perform dharma (religious, social and moral duties based on the idea of justice).
- Most Hindus believe that to gain moksha they must try to promote justice.
- The Hindu scriptures encourage Hindus to be concerned for others and to work for justice.
- The Hindu belief in ahimsa (non-violence) also encourages justice because the rich treating the poor badly is a form of violence.
- The great Hindu leader Mahatma Gandhi based his campaign for the independence of India from British rule on the Hindu idea of justice. He also developed the idea of sarvodaya (welfare for all) from the Hindu concept of justice.
- Hindu gurus and swamis teach that people's souls are improved if they treat other people justly.

Topic 4.4.4 Why justice is important for Sikhs

Key points

Justice is important for Sikhs because it is taught in the Guru Granth Sahib and all the Gurus worked for justice. Sikhism teaches that God is just and justice comes from God. The Rahit Maryada teaches that it is the duty of Sikhs to work for justice and remove injustice.

Evaluation questions

Evaluation questions will only ask you to refer to one religion, so you would be best just to use Christianity in answering evaluation questions, although you could use extra reasons from the other religion you have studied.

Main points

Justice is important for Sikhs because:

- The Guru Granth Sahib teaches that justice is an attribute of God. God is just and is the source of all justice.
- Sikhism teaches that it is the duty of Sikhs to bring God's justice into the world.
- Sikhs believe that human beings are imperfect and their justice is imperfect. Often justice systems favour the rich and powerful. Sikhs believe this is wrong and that Sikhs should work to bring God's justice into the world.
- The Rahit Maryada teaches that Sikhs should work for justice.
- Sikhism teaches that while unjust people can escape the human judge, they cannot escape from the Court of God. At the end of people's lives, God will give full justice to everyone.
- All the Gurus worked for justice and Sikhs should follow their example.

Topic 4.5 The nature of capital punishment

Main points

Capital punishment is punishment which takes away the criminal's life. This process is called the death penalty (execution). A crime which can be punished by the death penalty is called a capital offence. The UK abolished the death penalty in 1970.

Non-religious arguments in favour of capital punishment

- If people know they will die if they murder someone, it will put most people off murdering so there will be fewer murders.
- Murderers and terrorists threaten society, and the best way to protect society from them is to take away their lives.
- Human life is the most important thing there is and the value of human life can only be shown by giving those who take human life the worst possible punishment.
- Retribution is a major part of punishment and the only retribution for murder is the death penalty.

Non-religious arguments against capital punishment

- No court system can be sure that the correct verdict is always given. Wrongly convicted people can be released from prison, but not if they have been executed.
- Statistics of countries with the death penalty and those without the death penalty show that, if anything, those countries which do not use the death penalty have a lower murder rate.
- Murderers who know they are going to be killed if caught are more likely to kill more people to avoid being caught.
- Murderers often regard life imprisonment as worse than death as they try to commit suicide (for example, Harold Shipman and Ian Brady).

Key points

Capital punishment is punishment which takes the life of the criminal. Some people think it is a good idea because it takes a life for a life and deters people from murdering others. Some people think it is a bad punishment because there is evidence that it does not deter and trial mistakes can lead to innocent people being killed for crimes they did not commit.

Evaluation questions

You may be required to argue for and against capital punishment as an effective form of punishment.

1. To argue that it is, you should use any of the arguments in favour of capital punishment given above left.

2. To argue against, you should use any of the arguments against capital punishment given on the left.

Topic 4.6 Different attitudes to capital punishment among Christians

Key points

Many Christians think capital punishment is wrong because of the teachings of Jesus.

Some Christians agree with capital punishment to keep order in society because it is the teaching of the Church.

Evaluation questions

You may be required to argue for and against capital punishment being acceptable to religious people.

1. To argue for, you should use the points on the right for why some Christians believe capital punishment can be used.

2. To argue against, you could use the points above right for why most Christians believe capital punishment is un-Christian.

Main points

There are different attitudes among Christians towards capital punishment.

Many Christians believe that capital punishment is un-Christian, and that Christians should never use capital punishment. They believe this because:

- Jesus came to save (reform) sinners, but you cannot reform a dead person.
- Jesus said that an eye for an eye and a tooth for a tooth is wrong for Christians.
- Christianity teaches that all life is sacred; if abortion and euthanasia are wrong so is capital punishment.
- Most Christian Churches have made statements condemning capital punishment.

Some Christians believe that capital punishment can be used. They believe this because:

- The Bible gives the death penalty as the punishment for various offences.
- The Roman Catholic Church and the Church of England have not cancelled their statements that capital punishment can be used by the state.
- The Christian Church itself used capital punishment in the past for the crime of heresy (not believing official Church teachings).
- Christian thinkers such as St Thomas Aquinas said that the protection of society is a more important part of punishment than the reform of the criminal and they believed that capital punishment prevents murder and keeps order in society.

Topic 4.7.1 Different attitudes to capital punishment in Islam

Main points

Islam allows capital punishment for three offences: murder, adultery and Muslims who abandon Islam (apostasy).

Most Muslims agree with capital punishment because:
- It is a punishment set down by God in the Qur'an.
- Muhammad made several statements agreeing with capital punishment for murder, adultery and apostasy.
- Muhammad sentenced people to death for murder when he was ruler of Madinah.
- The Shari'ah says that capital punishment is the punishment for murder, adultery and apostasy.

Some Muslims do not agree with capital punishment because:
- It is recommended by the Qur'an, but is not compulsory.
- The Shari'ah says that the family of a murder victim can accept blood money from the murderer instead of death.
- They agree with the non-religious arguments against capital punishment (see Topic 4.5, page 67).

As you only need to study one religion, you should only learn one of the four topics on pages 69–71 – the religion you have studied at school.

Key points

Most Muslims agree with capital punishment because it is the punishment for certain crimes in the Qur'an. Some Muslims do not agree with capital punishment, because it is not compulsory in the Shari'ah, and for non-religious reasons.

Evaluation questions

Evaluation questions will only ask you to refer to one religion, so you would be best just to use Christianity in answering evaluation questions, although you could use extra reasons from Islam.

Topic 4.7.2 Different attitudes to capital punishment in Judaism

As you only need to study one religion, you should only learn one of the four topics on pages 69–71 – the religion you have studied at school.

Key points

Most Jews agree with capital punishment because it is approved by the Torah, and they think it will deter criminals. Some Jews think capital punishment is wrong because of what the Mishnah says.

Evaluation questions

Evaluation questions will only ask you to refer to one religion, so you would be best just to use Christianity in answering evaluation questions, although you could use extra reasons from Judaism.

Main points

Most Jews agree with capital punishment, but only if there is no possibility of reforming the murderer. They believe this because:

- The Torah says that capital punishment should be used for certain crimes.
- The Talmud says capital punishment can be used but with many restrictions.
- The basis of punishment is the protection of society and so murderers who will always be a danger to society should be executed.
- They believe capital punishment should be used if it will deter people from becoming a threat to society.

Some Jews do not agree with capital punishment because:

- The Mishnah seems to be against capital punishment.
- They agree with the non-religious arguments against capital punishment (see Topic 4.5, page 67).
- They believe the teachings of the Torah and Tenakh need updating and do not apply to today because of the non-religious arguments against capital punishment (see Topic 4.5, page 67).

Topic 4.7.3 Different attitudes to capital punishment in Hinduism

Main points

Most Hindus agree with capital punishment for murderers. They believe this because:

- The Vedas say that ahimsa does not apply to criminals.
- The Laws of Manu say that a Hindu can kill someone to maintain social order.
- The Vahara Purana says that a king can execute criminals to restore the correct dharma.
- They believe capital punishment deters murderers and protects society.

Some Hindus do not believe in capital punishment because:

- They believe execution is killing which gives bad karma and delays moksha.
- They believe ahimsa means no violence to anyone, even murderers.
- They accept the non-religious arguments against capital punishment (see Topic 4.5, page 67).

As you only need to study one religion, you should only learn one of the four topics on pages 69–71 – the religion you have studied at school.

Key points

Most Hindus believe capital punishment should be used for murderers because that is the teaching of the Law of Manu. Some Hindus disagree with capital punishment because of the teachings of ahimsa and karma and non-religious arguments.

Topic 4.7.4 Different attitudes to capital punishment in Sikhism

Main points

Most Sikhs are opposed to capital punishment because:

- The Sikh religion says all human beings have divine dignity, therefore none should be executed.
- There are no clear instructions on capital punishment in the Guru Granth Sahib.
- The Ten Gurus appear to have been against capital punishment.
- Killing in cold blood is banned by Sikhism.

Some Sikhs agree with capital punishment because:

- If there is no specific Sikh teaching, capital punishment must be allowed.
- They agree with the non-religious arguments for capital punishment (see Topic 4.5, page 67).

Key points

Most Sikhs are opposed to capital punishment because there are Sikh teachings against killing in cold blood. Some Sikhs agree with capital punishment because there are no clear instructions in the scriptures.

Evaluation questions

Evaluation questions will only ask you to refer to one religion, so you would be best just to use Christianity in answering evaluation questions, although you could use extra reasons from the other religion you have studied.

Topic 4.8 Laws on drugs and alcohol

Key points

The law bans smoking in public and workplaces and says tobacco products cannot be sold to under-eighteens. Alcohol cannot be sold to under-eighteens, or drunk by under-fives. All classified drugs are illegal. Class A drugs (such as heroin and cocaine) have the most severe penalties.

Evaluation questions

You may be required to argue for and against having laws to control/ban drugs. As any such questions will require knowledge of the social and health problems, the advice is given after Topic 4.9 (page 73).

Main points

UK laws on tobacco

- It is illegal to sell cigarettes, cigars, tobacco, etc. to anyone under eighteen years of age.
- All tobacco packs must have large health warnings and shocking picture warnings about the effects of smoking.
- All adverts and sponsorship for tobacco products are banned.
- It is against the law to smoke in all indoor public places, workplaces, football grounds and all parts of railway stations.

UK laws on alcohol

- It is illegal to give an alcoholic drink to a child under five years of age.
- Children under sixteen can go into a pub with adult supervision, but cannot have any alcoholic drinks. However, children can be banned if the pub has had problems.
- Young people aged sixteen or seventeen can drink beer, wine or cider with a meal, if it is bought by an adult and they are accompanied by an adult.
- It is against the law for anyone under eighteen to buy alcohol anywhere.

UK laws on illegal drugs

Class A, B and C drugs are termed as controlled substances and it is an offence:

- to possess a controlled substance unlawfully
- to possess a controlled substance with intent
- to supply or offer to supply a controlled drug
- to allow your premises to be used for drug taking.

The police have special powers to stop, detain and search people if they think they have a controlled drug.

Topic 4.9 Social and health problems caused by drugs and alcohol

Main points

Drugs and alcohol are controlled by law because they cause so many social and health problems.

Health problems caused by tobacco

- Smoking increases the risk of at least fifty medical conditions.
- Various cancers; coronary heart disease; stroke, chronic bronchitis and emphysema can be caused by smoking.
- In men, smoking can cause impotence (it limits the blood supply to the penis).
- The babies of mothers who smoke during pregnancy have a lower birth weight, are weaker and may not develop normally.

Health problems caused by alcohol

- If you drink heavily, you have an increased risk of developing serious health conditions such as liver problems, stomach disorders, heart disease and some cancers.
- Heavy drinking can lead to alcohol dependence (**addiction**).
- About one in seven road deaths is caused by the effects of drinking alcohol.

Health problems caused by drugs

- The physical health of users can be damaged by the toxic effects of a drug.
- Many deaths of drug users are caused by infections, liver disease or intentional self-harm.
- Heavy users often have psychiatric illnesses.

Key points

Smoking can cause many bad health effects and deaths which cause problems for families, employers, etc. Alcohol causes many health problems such as liver disease and alcoholism. It also causes major social problems as people behave violently and irrationally when drunk. Drug abuse can cause addiction and death. It also causes criminal gang problems and stealing to fund the habit.

Evaluation questions

You may be required to argue for and against tobacco, alcohol, drugs being controlled by laws.

1. To argue for, you could use any of the points on pages 73–74 about the health and social problems they cause.

2. To argue against, you could use such reasons as:
   - A country like the Netherlands which has decriminalised some 'soft' drugs such as cannabis seems to have fewer drug problems.
   - Laws which prohibited alcohol use in the past, such as in the USA in the 1920s, caused problems with organised crime.
   - It should be an individual choice as to whether to use tobacco, alcohol or drugs as they only affect an individual's body.

Social problems caused by drugs and alcohol

Tobacco

- The suffering of families of smokers watching their loved ones die slowly from diseases they would not have had if they had never smoked.

Alcohol

- Social disorder in town centres as seen on Friday and Saturday evenings.
- Forty-one per cent of all deaths from falls, thirty per cent of drownings, twenty-five per cent of boating deaths, and fifty per cent of fire deaths are caused by the effects of alcohol.
- Seventy per cent of murder victims and forty per cent of rape offenders had been drinking at the time of the incident.
- Fifty per cent of those who commit sex abuse crimes also abuse alcohol.

Illegal drugs

- All drug dealers are criminals and this leads to violence between different gangs of suppliers.
- The high cost of maintaining a heroin or cocaine habit forces users into a life of crime.
- Some users become violent under a drug's influence.

Nevertheless, statistics show that the use of illegal drugs fell from 12.1 per cent of adults in 1998 to 10.5 per cent in 2006.

Topic 4.10 Different attitudes to drugs and alcohol in Christianity

Main points

All Christians are against drugs because they are illegal and they abuse the body, which is God's temple. There are two different attitudes to tobacco and alcohol among Christians.

Most Christians believe that the correct approach to alcohol and tobacco is moderation because:

- The first miracle that Jesus performed was changing water into wine at a wedding feast.
- St Paul said that Christians could drink in moderation.
- Jesus used bread and wine at his Last Supper and told his disciples to continue the tradition.
- Most Churches use alcoholic wine in their communion services, so Christians must be able to drink wine in moderation.
- Moderation is the teaching of the Catholic Church in the Catechism.

Some Christians (especially Pentecostals, members of the Salvation Army and many Methodists) do not drink alcoholic drinks, and do not smoke because:

- They believe that taking tobacco or alcohol is abusing God's temple (our bodies).
- There are passages in the Bible warning against drunkenness which they consider sufficient reason for keeping away from the use of alcohol, tobacco or narcotics.
- The Bible also teaches that consumption of alcohol damages judgement, inflames passions and invites violence.
- Many of these Christians are involved in working with alcoholics and know how they need to be supported by others refusing alcohol (recovering alcoholics cannot have any alcohol at all).

Key points

All Christians are against drugs because they are illegal and abuse the body which is God's temple. Most Christians accept the use of alcohol and tobacco in moderation because this is the teaching of the Church. Jesus drank wine and wine is used for communion in many Churches. Some Christians believe they should not touch wine or tobacco because of their harmful social and health effects and because the Bible shows concern for the harmful effects of alcohol.

Evaluation questions

You may be required to argue for and against religious people drinking alcohol.

- To argue for, you could use the reasons above left why some Christians believe in moderation.
- To argue against, you could use the reasons on the left why some Christians do not drink alcoholic drinks.

Topic 4.11.1 Attitudes to drugs and alcohol in Islam

As you only need to study one religion, you should only learn one of the four topics on pages 76–79 – the religion you have studied at school.

Key points

Islam forbids the use of drugs or alcohol because they are banned in the Qur'an and in the hadith of the Prophet and they cause much harm.

Tobacco is disapproved of, but not banned.

Evaluation questions

Evaluation questions will only ask you to refer to one religion, so you would be best just to use Christianity in answering evaluation questions, although you could use extra reasons from Islam.

Main points

Alcohol and drugs are prohibited for Muslims (haram) because:

- The Qur'an says that intoxicants are a means by which Satan tries to keep people from God and from saying their prayers.
- The Prophet Muhammad said that every intoxicant is forbidden to Muslims (khamr).
- Muslim lawyers say taking drugs or alcohol is a form of suicide because you are harming your body, and suicide is forbidden.
- Muhammad said several times that Muslims must not drink alcohol, and must also have nothing to do with the production or sale of alcohol.

Tobacco is regarded as haram by some Muslims because it harms the body, but Muslim lawyers have declared it makruh (disliked) because it is not mentioned by the Qur'an or Muhammad.

Topic 4.11.2 Attitudes to drugs and alcohol in Judaism

Main points

All Jewish people are against the use of illegal drugs because:

- The Torah teaches that being addicted to physical pleasures and doing anything to support a habit is wrong.
- Using drugs makes it difficult to pray, fulfil mitzvot and learn the Torah properly.
- Young people using drugs stops them from honouring their parents, because parents will be upset.
- The Torah says, 'You shall be holy' so Jewish people should not take drugs.

Since the discoveries of the effects of smoking on health, Jewish people are advised not to smoke because of the mitzvah to be holy.

Most Jewish people believe alcohol should be used in moderation because:

- The Tenakh speaks in praise of wine as a substance that 'gladdens the human heart'.
- The use of wine is required in Shabbat and festivals.
- Drunkenness is condemned in the Tenakh and anyone under the influence of alcohol is forbidden to pray until sober.
- The command of the Torah to be holy means that Jewish people must be moderate in their use of alcohol.

As you only need to study one religion, you should only learn one of the four topics on pages 76–79 – the religion you have studied at school.

Key points

Judaism is against the use of drugs because they lead to addiction and prevent the keeping of the mitzvot. It is also against smoking because Jewish people should not harm their bodies. It allows the use of alcohol in moderation because the Tenakh praises wine, and wine plays a central part in Jewish rituals such as Kiddush.

Evaluation questions

Evaluation questions will only ask you to refer to one religion, so you would be best just to use Christianity in answering evaluation questions, although you could use extra reasons from Judaism.

Topic 4.11.3 Attitudes to drugs and alcohol in Hinduism

As you only need to study one religion, you should only learn one of the four topics on pages 76–79 – the religion you have studied at school.

Key points

- Some Hindus do not allow the use of drugs, tobacco or alcohol because of the teachings of the scriptures and the danger that they may make it impossible to gain moksha.
- Other Hindus allow them in moderation because they help in remembering God, and some goddesses are shown drinking wine.

Evaluation questions

Evaluation questions will only ask you to refer to one religion, so you would be best just to use Christianity in answering evaluation questions, although you could use extra reasons from Hinduism.

Main points

Some Hindus do not allow drugs, tobacco or alcohol because:

- The smriti scriptures say drinking wine is one of the Five Great Sins.
- It is said that Brahma and Krishna cursed wine because of its harmful effects.
- The use of drugs, tobacco or alcohol may lead people away from God, making moksha impossible.
- Many Hindu gurus and swamis take a vow to refrain from alcohol, drugs and tobacco as they cloud the soul.

In the Hindu tantric tradition, drugs, tobacco and alcohol are allowed in moderation because:

- There are tantric rituals which use wine.
- The joy that one can experience from alcohol is used as an aid to the remembrance of the joy of communing with God.
- Feminine aspects of God are sometimes shown enjoying the intoxication of wine.

However, the tantric tradition condemns drunkenness as it may lead to the absence of the remembrance of God.

Topic 4.11.4 Attitudes to drugs and alcohol in Sikhism

Main points

Sikhism does not allow the use of alcohol, drugs or tobacco because:

- One of the rules of the Khalsa is never to use tobacco or other drugs.
- The Guru Granth Sahib says that Sikhs should avoid wine and marijuana.
- Guru Nanak said that his followers should avoid all intoxicants.
- Sikhs are taught to avoid everything that harms the body or the mind. This means that all drugs are forbidden.
- The aim of Sikhism is to move from being manmukh to becoming gurmukh, but the use of alcohol, drugs and tobacco drives a person away from the spiritual realities of life (gurmukh).

As you only need to study one religion, you should only learn one of the four topics on pages 76–79 – the religion you have studied at school.

Key points

Sikhs are taught not to use alcohol, drugs or tobacco because it is the teaching of Guru Nanak and the Guru Granth Sahib and one of the rules of the Khalsa.

Evaluation questions

Evaluation questions will only ask you to refer to one religion, so you would be best just to use Christianity in answering evaluation questions, although you could use extra reasons from Sikhism.

How to answer questions on Section 4

You should already know the basics about how to answer questions from Section 1, pages 16–18, but here is an answer to a whole question on Section 4 with a commentary to help you.

Question a)
What is addiction? (2 marks)

Answer

Like what you get to drugs.

> One mark for a partially correct answer.

Answer

A recurring compulsion to engage in an activity regardless of its bad effects.

> Two marks for a correct definition.

Question b)
Do you think laws need to be just?
Give TWO reasons for your point of view. (4 marks)

Answer

I do think they need to be just because if laws are unjust, then they are not fulfilling their purpose ...

> One mark for a reason.

... which is to make sure that people are rewarded for their work, the weak are protected, etc.

> Two marks because the reason is developed.

Also, if a law is unjust, people will not obey it ...

> Three marks because a second reason is given.

... and will campaign against the law, causing trouble in society.

> Four marks because the second reason is developed.

> Total = four marks. Remember! Response questions are really like part (i) of an evaluation question where you only have to give two reasons. To answer a response question, you should just use two reasons from the point of view you agree with in the evaluation questions advice for a topic.

Question c)
Choose one religion other than Christianity and explain why justice is important in that religion.
(8 marks)

Answer

Justice is important for Muslims because the Qur'an says God is just, and if God is just, Muslims should be just.

> LEVEL 1: two marks for a reason for one attitude expressed in basic English.

Also, Muslims believe it is part of their role as vice-gerents of God's creation to treat all people fairly, and so they should promote justice.

> LEVEL 2: by giving a second reason for the attitude, the answer goes up to level 2 and because the answer is written in clear English it would gain four marks.

Furthermore, the Shari'ah (the holy law of Islam) is based on justice for everyone with everyone being treated equally. The Shari'ah should be the law for all Muslims and so justice must be important.

> LEVEL 3: by adding another attitude with a reason the answer moves up to level 3 and because the answer is written in a clear style of English with some use of specialist vocabulary (Qur'an, vice-gerent, God's creation, Shari'ah, holy law) it would gain six marks.

Finally, Islam teaches that it is unjust to be involved in the charging of interest (riba) because it takes money from the poor and gives it to the rich. This shows the importance of justice as Muslims cannot have anything to do with interest, which causes them problems when living in Western society.

> LEVEL 4: by adding a further reason for the second attitude, the answer moves up to level 4 and because it is written in a clear and correct style of English with extra specialist vocabulary (unjust, riba, Western society) it would gain eight marks – full marks.

Question d)

'Capital punishment is the best punishment for murderers.'

(i) Do you agree? Give reasons for your opinion. (3 marks)

(ii) Give reasons why some people may disagree with you. (3 marks)

In your answer, you should refer to at least one religion.

Answer

(i) I do not agree because no court system can ever be sure that the correct verdict is always given. Wrongly convicted people can be released from prison, but not if they have been executed.

> One mark for a personal opinion with a reason.

Also, the statistics of countries with the death penalty and those without the death penalty show that, if anything, those countries which do not use the death penalty have a lower murder rate.

> Another reason is given so it moves up to two marks.

It also seems to be the case that murderers who know they are going to be killed if caught are more likely to kill more people to avoid being caught. Finally, murderers often regard life imprisonment as worse than death as they try to commit suicide (for example, Harold Shipman and Ian Brady).

> The answer now gives another two reasons for the opinion, so it moves up to three marks. The last reason cannot gain any marks, but it can be useful to give four reasons (if you have time), just in case one is incorrect.

(ii) Some Christians would disagree with me because the Bible gives the death penalty as the punishment for various offences and they think the Bible is the word of God.

> One mark for a reason why some people might disagree.

Also, Christian thinkers such as St Thomas Aquinas said that the protection of society is a more important part of punishment than the reform of the criminal and some Christians believe that capital punishment prevents murder and keeps order in society.

> Another reason is given so it moves up to two marks.

Muslims might also disagree because the Shari'ah says that capital punishment is the punishment for murder, adultery and apostasy.

> The answer now gives another reason for some people disagreeing, so it moves up to three marks.

> This answer to question d) can gain full marks because part (ii) refers to Christianity and Islam.

SECTION 4 TEST

SECTION 4: Crime and punishment

Answer both questions

1. a) What is rehabilitation? (2 marks)

   b) Do you think justice is important for Christians? Give two reasons for your point of view. (4 marks)

   c) Choose one religion other than Christianity and explain the attitude of its followers to alcohol. (8 marks)

   d) 'Punishment should be an eye for an eye and a tooth for a tooth.'
   - (i) Do you agree? Give reasons for your opinion. (3 marks)
   - (ii) Give reasons why some people may disagree with you. (3 marks)

   (Total: 20 marks)

2. a) What is justice? (2 marks)

   b) Do you think punishment should try to reform criminals? Give two reasons for your point of view. (4 marks)

   c) Choose one religion other than Christianity and explain why some of its followers approve of capital punishment and some do not. (8 marks)

   d) 'We don't need laws on drugs and alcohol.'
   - (i) Do you agree? Give reasons for your opinion. (3 marks)
   - (ii) Give reasons why some people may disagree with you. (3 marks)

   In your answer you should refer to at least one religion.

   (Total: 20 marks)

You should now use the mark scheme in the Appendix, page 83 to mark your answers, and the self-help tables in the Appendix, pages 84–85 to see how you can improve your performance. If you need more help with the mark scheme for these questions, go to www.hoddereducation.co.uk/religionandsociety

Appendix

Mark scheme for section tests

a) questions (2 marks)

Use the key words list on page 4 for Section 1, page 20 for Section 2, page 41 for Section 3, page 60 for Section 4. Award 2 marks for a correct answer.

b) questions (4 marks)

- A personal response with one brief reason award 1 mark.
- A personal response with two brief reasons award 2 marks.
- A personal response with one developed reason award 2 marks.
- For a personal response with two reasons with one developed award 3 marks.
- For a personal response with two developed reasons award 4 marks.

c) questions (8 marks)

- Level 1: for a brief reason in basic English award 2 marks.
- Level 2: for two brief reasons in basic English award 4 marks.
- Level 3: for three brief reasons written in a clear style with some specialist vocabulary award 5 or 6 marks depending on the Quality of Written Communication (QWC).
- Level 4: for four brief reasons written in a clear and correct style of English with a correct use of specialist vocabulary award 7 or 8 marks depending on the QWC.

d) questions (6 marks)

Part (i)

- One reason award 1 mark.
- Two reasons award 2 marks.
- Three reasons award 3 marks.

Part (ii)

- One reason award 1 mark.
- Two reasons award 2 marks.
- Three reasons award 3 marks.

How to improve your performance

When you have completed each test, make a copy of this table and fill it in using your marks.

	Question 1	Question 2
1. How many marks did I get for question a)?		
2. How many marks did I get for question b)? If less than 4:		
• Did I forget to give reasons?		
• Did I forget to develop my reasons?		
3. How many marks did I get for question c)? If less than 8:		
• Did I forget to use specialist vocabulary?		
• Did I describe instead of explain?		
• Did I misunderstand the question?		
• Did I give too few reasons?		
• Did I forget about the Quality of Written Communication?		
4. How many marks did I get for question d)? If less than 6:		
• Did I forget to make one point of view be from one religion?		
• Did I forget to use information from the book?		
• Did I give too few reasons for part (i)?		
• Did I give too few reasons for part (ii)?		

Now use your completed table to complete a copy of this sheet which will show you what you need to do to improve:

HOW TO IMPROVE MY PERFORMANCE

Using the mark table, circle the targets that apply to you.

1. Question a)

Marks	Target
4 or more marks	Make sure I still know all the key words
3 or fewer marks	Learn the key words more thoroughly

2. Question b)

Marks	Target
Yes to bullet point 1	Remember to give reasons for my opinion
Yes to bullet point 2	Make sure I write developed reasons for my opinion

3. Question c)

Marks	Target
Yes to bullet point 1	Remember to use the key words in my part c) answers Learn and use specialist terms
Yes to bullet point 2	Practise understanding questions so that I explain why or how
Yes to bullet point 3	Make sure you read the question carefully and answer what it asks for, not what you want it to ask for
Yes to bullet point 4	Make sure to give four reasons
Yes to bullet point 5	Remember to take care with spelling and punctuation Remember not to use bullet points

4. Question d)

Marks	Target
Yes to bullet point 1	Make sure that either your own point of view or the one which disagrees with you is from a named religion
Yes to bullet point 2	Make sure to use reasons from the Revision Guide
Yes to bullet point 3 or 4	Make sure to give three reasons for each part